# ONCE
## UPON A TIME

### BEHIND THE MAGIC

Once Upon a Time: Behind the Magic
ISBN: 978-1-78276-029-0

Published by Titan Books.
A division of Titan Publishing Group Ltd, 144 Southwark Street, London SE1 0UP.

A CIP catalogue record for this title is available from the British Library.
First edition: October 2013.
10 9 8 7 6 5 4 3 2

Printed in China.
Titan Books.

**TITAN BOOKS**
Collection Editor: **Neil Edwards**
Collection Designer: **Daniel Bura**
Collection Senior Editor: **Natalie Clubb**

Production Supervisors:
**Jackie Flook, Kelly Fenlon**

Art Director: **Oz Browne**
Studio Manager: **Selina Juneja**
Publishing Manager: **Darryl Tothill**
Publishing Director: **Chris Teather**
Operations Director: **Leigh Baulch**
Executive Director: **Vivian Cheung**
Publisher: **Nick Landau**

**ACKNOWLEDGMENTS**
**TITAN WOULD LIKE TO THANK...**
The cast and crew of *Once Upon a Time*, Melissa Harling-Walendy, Marielle Henault, Samantha Thomas, Tessa Leigh Williams, and Melanie Braunstein for their help in the making of this volume.

abc studios    abc

# The Story So Far...

# Cast

# Crew

# A Long, Long

Words: Paul Terry

FANS OF ABC STUDIOS' EPIC
ISLAND SAGA *LOST* WOULD
HAVE ALREADY BEEN FAMILIAR
WITH THE AMAZING WORK
OF WRITING DUO EDWARD
KITSIS AND ADAM HOROWITZ,
BUT *ONCE UPON A TIME* IS A
DIFFERENT STORY ALTOGETHER.
HAVING CREATED, NURTURED,
AND CAST THE SPELL FOR THE
SERIES – A TASK THAT HAS
ITS OWN MAGICAL TALE OF
PATIENCE AND REWARD – THE
CO-CREATORS/EXECUTIVE
PRODUCERS FLASH BACK TO
THE ORIGINS OF THEIR MODERN
FANTASY ADVENTURE...

# Time Ago...

**C**reating a brand new show that balances a huge cast, multiple timelines, adventure, thrills and humor – but most importantly, engaging characters – would terrify most. However, Edward Kitsis and Adam Horowitz are more than familiar with such weighty responsibility. After all, they crafted *Tron: Legacy* (a film that bore the pressure of 28 years of mythological fan expectation since the first movie) and served the ever-complex *Lost* island for its six-season run as writers and executive producers. But time is a funny thing in television. Often, ideas hatch and then grow into hits long after their inception. In the case of *Once Upon a Time,* for example, it was nearly a decade-long process, something that the creators of the show explain was nothing but a blessing...

"The idea for *Once* originated nine years ago, when we were coming off of *Felicity*," Kitsis explains, referring to the duo's time on the hit college drama created by J.J. Abrams and Matt Reeves. "We were thinking about the kind of show that we wanted to write. We wanted to do something that would allow us to do all the things we love." In a strange foreshadowing of where their careers would take them next, Kitsis continues, "In a lot of ways, the idea was similar to *Lost*, as far as one week could be funny, one week could be scary, and the next week could be romantic. We were sitting around and talking about fairy tales, and how they're important to us, because they were the first stories we'd ever heard as children. That gave us the basic idea for the show."

From the seeds of crafting a show that balanced all these genres and tones, it led the writers to a classic fairy tale trope that inspired some great innovation and invention. "We started talking about how hard it would be being the Evil Queen, because you were stuck in a place with happy endings, so everything you do fails. You get an oven working in a gingerbread house, and the witch can't kill the two kids. So we thought, 'What's the one place where she could win?' That place? It would be *our* world."

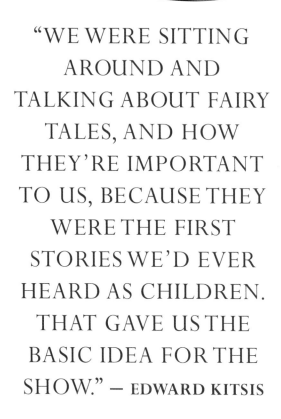

> "WE WERE SITTING AROUND AND TALKING ABOUT FAIRY TALES, AND HOW THEY'RE IMPORTANT TO US, BECAUSE THEY WERE THE FIRST STORIES WE'D EVER HEARD AS CHILDREN. THAT GAVE US THE BASIC IDEA FOR THE SHOW." — EDWARD KITSIS

Even nine years ago, one character was always key. "We had the idea of Emma, although she didn't have a name yet – she was just Snow White and Prince Charming's daughter," explains Kitsis. "But we were young, and it was a very different time in Hollywood. We took it around to a few people, but they all passed on it."

The writers still ended up writing mysterious tales about characters in an unknown land, an experience that they're certain helped evolve *Once Upon a Time* into the show it is today. "I think being on *Lost* is what really made it work. Adam and I always say how it was like a nine-year writers' block on this particular project. When we got to *Lost*, we realized that maybe there could be a different way of telling our story. So when *Lost* ended, and we still liked this idea of ours, we pitched it and ABC liked it," smiles Kitsis.

In many ways, their experience is a good lesson for young writers to learn: patience. "We'd been thinking about it and marinading it for almost nine years, and this is when it all came together. So much about it is timing, and we look back and think, 'Thank goodness it took this long,' because I don't think we would've been able to do it back then."

Visual effects are such a key element for *Once*, to sell the notion of other realms and magical powers effectively, and Adam Horowitz agrees that nowadays, it's within budgetary reach. "Technology is so much better today," he explains. "I think a lot of the stuff that we do on the show would have been cost prohibitive, even five years ago. There's stuff available now that's just amazing. However, for us, it's always about making the effects appear real." Kitsis concurs, explaining, "Even if we're doing a green-screen sequence, we always want to have a real table or a real chair there. It's important that the actors have something real to play with, so that they're not just surrounded with green. For us, it is always about balancing the effects with the practical." The locations where *Once* shoots have even added an extra realism that they weren't intending. "Vancouver always looks so great. When it was snowing in the 'Red-Handed' episode, all of that snow was real," Kitsis says.

With a premise that casts a wide-angle lens across the entire spectrum of story book characters, the co-creators knew they needed to have a central character from where *Once*'s saga would stem. Their decision from nine years ago remained the same. "We always knew that we wanted the Snow White story to be at the center of the show, and that was sort of ground zero for fairy tales for us," explains Horowitz. "The other characters for Season One were then out-growths of that classic story. The fun idea for us was, 'How can we mash up these stories, and take characters like Snow White and put them with characters like Red Riding Hood and Rumplestiltskin?'"

With an almost endless list of classic characters and fairy tale arcs to mine, nearly all of their wish list came true for the first season – except one. "The only character that we wanted to be part of the show but weren't able to do for Season One, because of a rights issue, was Captain Hook," Horowitz reveals. "But now in Season Two we're finally getting to venture into the *Peter Pan* mythology. That was something that we always wanted to be a part of the show. Luckily, that sorted itself out over the course of Season One, so we're now able to use

# A Day In The Life

***Once* co-creator/ executive producer Adam Horowitz explains what he and Edward Kitsis go through to bring each episode to life...**

"It takes a long time for each episode to happen. Before the season even starts we spend a number of weeks with the writers, talking about the 'big picture' stuff. For example, what we wanted Season Two to be, talking about our big plans that we have for the show overall, and trying to outline what pieces of that story we'd touch on in the second season. Then we all reconvened at the beginning of the summer last year, to start talking about the specifics of the episodes. It starts with what the episode is going to be about, and we spend a few weeks in the writers' room hashing out the plot. We then send a writer off to write an outline. From the outline we go to a script, and that's usually another couple of weeks. After that, there's about eight or nine days of prep time, where we're prepping the episode before it shoots, and then there's an eight-day shoot for that episode. When *that's* done, there's another four to eight weeks of post-production, depending on where we are in the season. So from the initial 'What is episode four gonna be about?' conversation to the locked cut, it can be a two or three-month process."

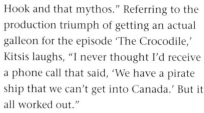

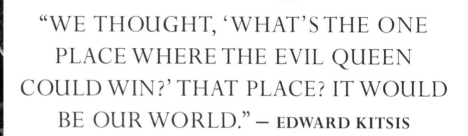

Hook and that mythos." Referring to the production triumph of getting an actual galleon for the episode 'The Crocodile,' Kitsis laughs, "I never thought I'd receive a phone call that said, 'We have a pirate ship that we can't get into Canada.' But it all worked out."

Thanks to their time on *Lost*, the duo were more than familiar with working on a TV show that requires a delicate balancing of multiple characters and intriguing plot. Although each new project brings its own unique challenges, the ultimate goal for the writers-producers remained the same throughout *Once*'s debut season. "The

> "WE THOUGHT, 'WHAT'S THE ONE PLACE WHERE THE EVIL QUEEN COULD WIN?' THAT PLACE? IT WOULD BE OUR WORLD." — EDWARD KITSIS

trickiest thing, in a lot of ways, to balance in Season One was telling the story of our main characters, but it was also about introducing new characters into the mix," says Kitsis. "You're trying to dig deeper and get people to love the characters from the pilot episode, but you're also trying to expand that world."

Horowitz agrees. "That's a tricky dance. For us, always, you don't ever want mythology to trump character. So the hardest thing about the show is making it simple, even if it's complicated. Even if it's in three timelines. As long as the general story is, 'Emma wants to save her son, Snow wants to get back to Charming, etc,' then it works. It's all about trying to take a big world, and making it simple."

Making and maintaining more than one big world brought its challenges. "The first season was also difficult, because you had magic, fairies, dwarves, and Rumplestiltskin turning things into gold. But, on the other hand, you had the other people who didn't know who they were, and the Storybrooke stories are

essentially based in real life," explains Kitsis. "So we are always trying to make the Storybrooke stories as exciting as the ones in a far away land where characters are slaying a beast."

With the chessboard set during a show's first season, Kitsis agrees that the follow-up year gives the writers a great opportunity to peel back more layers. "What's great for Season Two is that, where we introduced characters last year, we now get to dig deeper. We've done an Emma flashback, and now that 30-some episodes have aired, the audience really understands her more." With magic now in Storybrooke, it's also adding new layers to the storytelling. "It's really fun having magic in Storybrooke because it's great to be able to tell a story where Ruby turns into a wolf and no longer remembers it, and the town has to go after her," Horowitz smiles. "We love that juxtaposition between the modern world and the Enchanted Forest."

So do the fans, especially with how the first half of Season Two built to its mid-season cliffhangers. The dilemmas for *Once*'s eclectic

"WE ALWAYS KNEW THAT WE WANTED THE SNOW WHITE STORY TO BE AT THE CENTER OF THE SHOW, AND THAT WAS SORT OF GROUND ZERO FOR FAIRY TALES FOR US."

— ADAM HOROWITZ

# A Family Affair

**Once** co-creator/ executive producer Edward Kitsis reveals what reactions he hears the most from friends and family...

"It's less about any specific character. What I hear a lot is reactions to this sort of crazy, intertwined family, where you have Henry, with two mothers – both of whom have a very legitimate claim to being his mother – who are *also* part of the Charming family... with the Evil Queen who was the stepmother of Snow White... who is the mother of the *mother* of the kid! Just the way that that folds in on each other has been really fun for us to write. We love hearing from people about how they observe these relationships zig and zag."

"WHAT I THINK IS AN INTERESTING ARC IS THAT REGINA, WHO ENACTED A CURSE THAT CREATED A VOID IN HER HEART, CHOSE HENRY'S LIFE OVER THE CURSE." – ADAM HOROWITZ

collection of heroes, heroines, villains, and villainesses is entering even more intriguing realms, something which the duo are thrilled to capitalize on. "Cora and Hook make it to Storybrooke (in episode nine), and it's going to be really fun to see Hook in that town," says Kitsis. "What I think is an interesting arc," joins in Horowitz, "is that for Season One, Regina, who enacted a curse that created a void in her heart, chose Henry's life over the curse. She could've let Henry die, not told anyone about the sleeping

curse, not admitted to Emma that it was real, and then everything would've gone on as normal. But she chose to save Henry's life." Kitsis adds, "So this year you have Regina trying not to use magic and be a better person. But in the end it doesn't have the results that she was hoping for. Regina does find herself a bit broken by the end of the first nine episodes of this season. But as we know," he smiles, "her mother is more than ready to come and pick up the pieces..."

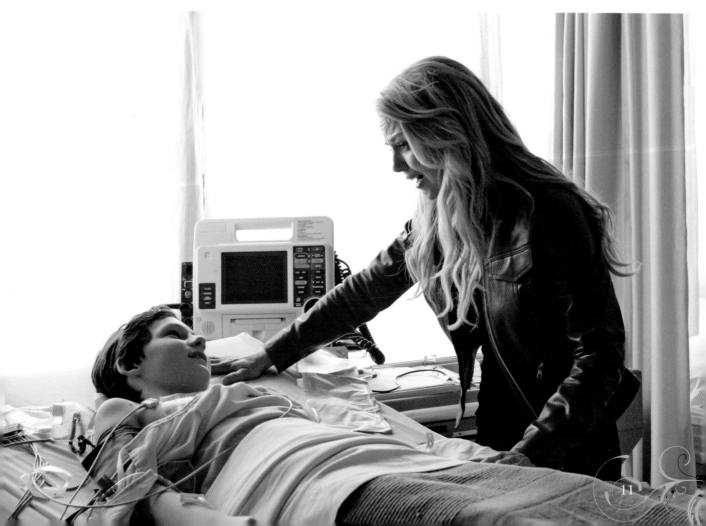

# PUREST SNOW

**LANDING THE ROLE OF SNOW WHITE ON *ONCE UPON A TIME* HAS BEEN A DREAM COME TRUE FOR ACTRESS GINNIFER GOODWIN. HERE, SHE TELLS US WHAT IT'S LIKE TO REINVENT SUCH AN ICONIC CHARACTER…**

Words: Tara Bennett

Fortunately for an actress who is playing one of the most famous fairy tale characters ever, Ginnifer Goodwin is a self-proclaimed enthusiast of classic Disney movies! Yes, the actress, who hails from Memphis, Tennessee and who fell in love with all things Disney as a kid landed perhaps the sweetest acting gig an über-fan could dream of: playing Snow White on *Once Upon a Time*. Not only is she playing the character that Walt Disney crafted his first feature–length animated film around back in 1937, but *Once Upon a Time* also features a whole gaggle of Walt-inspired variations on classic fairy tale characters who make up Fairy Tale Land and Storybrooke, Maine. The woman who played pretend princess as a little girl now gets to do it professionally and inspire a whole new generation of boys and girls.

It's a "pinch me" kind of existence that Goodwin tells us she is incredibly pleased to be living.

"It's funny because I feel that my love of Disney grew when I was first taken to visit the Magic Kingdom as a child," Goodwin reminisces. "My favorite films when I was very small were *Winnie the Pooh* and *Alice in Wonderland*. I really fell in love with Disney, in general, when my little sister [*Robot Chicken* animator Melissa Goodwin Shepherd] showed me her VHS tape of *The Little Mermaid*." Goodwin pauses before adding proudly, "Coincidentally, *The Little Mermaid* is why [Melissa] became an animator.

"At the time I was going through a phase where I felt like I was far too old and far too *mature* to watch what I called a 'cartoon,' so I resented being hijacked and being forced to watch a cartoon mermaid," Goodwin huffs with a faux dramatic sigh. "But after sobbing through the ending, I realized I was a Disneyphile. I feel like my eyes were opened to the world of Walt Disney's fairy tale storytelling more than it was about falling in love with the Grimm stories, or falling in love with the princesses. It was more that I became an acolyte to Walt and how he told stories, even though *The Little Mermaid* clearly wasn't a Walt [original]."

Goodwin says her love for Disney continued to bloom, and the films continued to be favorites with her family. "I went back with my mother and watched all the [Disney animated] originals because we own the entire library." She does admit Snow White was a favorite. "I gravitated towards Snow White, I think, for probably shallow aesthetic reasons," she laughs. "She is a brunette and I was brunette, and I was a kid, therefore I thought I could relate, not truly understanding the story. I don't feel like I can relate to Snow White in any real way, not the Disney version or the Grimm version. I think it was something far more simplistic in that I would dress up like her and go to school."

## From *Big Love* to True Love

Once Goodwin began to act professionally after graduating from Boston University's College of Fine Arts, she made a name for herself in high profile films like *Win a Date with Tad Hamilton!*, *Walk the Line*, *Mona Lisa Smile*, *He's Just Not That Into You* and *Something Borrowed*. However, audiences probably knew her best from her TV work, first in *Ed*, and then in HBO's polygamy drama, *Big Love*. And it's in TV that Goodwin got the opportunity to circle back to her Disney love when she was offered the role of Snow White in Eddy Kitsis and Adam Horowitz's revisionist fairy tale drama.

Fresh off a five-year run on *Big Love*, Goodwin remembers that she wasn't necessarily thinking about TV again, but the *Once Upon a Time* pilot was just too good to pass up. "I was intrigued by its uniqueness. No one has ever done anything like this on television before. I felt good about the creative part of the risk. I was also not looking at moving to another country [Canada]. I'm a homebody. I love living in Los Angeles. A lot of my family is here, my friends are here, and my life is here. It wasn't what I planned, but, ultimately, I just felt that

"NO ONE HAS EVER DONE ANYTHING LIKE THIS ON TELEVISION BEFORE. I FELT GOOD ABOUT THE CREATIVE PART OF THE RISK.

15

I would end up watching the show and loving it as an audience member, and I would be jealous if I wasn't part of it. I also really wanted to make something for my future children. *Big Love* is something my kids will *not* be able to watch until they are adults! I feel even the rom-coms I've made have been a bit dark, complicated and mature. This show is a way for me to be involved in a straight-up family project, and be proud of it and want to watch it myself."

However, she's quick to clarify that despite her love for classic Disney projects, she wasn't interested in doing a version of *Once Upon a Time* that was too straightforward. "I had no interest in duplicating the animated [*Snow White*]. I love the movie *Enchanted*, but I had no interest in making *Enchanted: the TV Series*. *Once Upon a Time* was somehow going to be grittier."

## Did You Know?

- As well as Ginnifer Goodwin, other actresses who have taken on the part of Snow White in other adaptations of the story include Elizabeth McGovern, Irene Cara, Halle Berry, Amanda Bynes, Kristin Kreuk, Lily Collins, and Kristen Stewart. In the classic 1937 Disney animation *Snow White and the Seven Dwarfs*, she was voiced by Adriana Caselotti.
- In the Brothers Grimm's first draft of the Snow White story, the Evil Queen character was Snow White's mother, not her stepmother. It is thought that changing her to Snow White's stepmother was done to make the story more palatable to children.
- The Brothers Grimm wrote another story, Snow White and Rose Red, but despite having a character with the same name, it has no connection to the better-known *Snow White* story.

"THE THING ABOUT SNOW WHITE IS THAT IT'S NOT SUPPOSED TO BE A STORY ABOUT AN INNOCENT BYSTANDER….IT'S SUPPOSED TO BE ABOUT A WOMAN WHOSE FATAL FLAW IS THE SAME AS HER EVIL STEPMOTHER'S."

## Cautionary Tales

Goodwin says figuring out how to play the different personalities of Snow and Mary Margaret was initially a challenge to crack, and she threw herself into researching the origins of Snow White for inspiration. "At first I watched every version of *Snow White* that's available: the ballet, the television episodes from various series, and every movie under the sun. I thought I would probably steal tidbits here and there, but I found nothing. I started reading *A Critical Analysis of Fairy Tales* and reading about fairy tales in a historical context. They were all cautionary tales and were meant to teach people of that time about very real-life issues. The thing about Snow White is that it's not supposed to be a story about an innocent bystander who is just so beautiful that her evil stepmother keeps trying to murder her," she laughs. "It's supposed to be about a woman whose fatal flaw is the same as her evil stepmother's. She can't refuse things like the stays for her corset, or the poisoned comb for her hair, or the beautiful apple, which alludes to sexual beauty. She is just the camera negative to the Evil Queen, but she navigates her vanity in a very different way. It's still there and it's the reason why she is ultimately killed

> "THE WOMEN CHARACTERS ON *ONCE* ARE SO EVOLVED AND COMPLICATED. THEIR RELATIONSHIPS ARE SO BEAUTIFUL."

momentarily. Realizing that changed everything and made me think long and hard about this woman's flaws and what it would mean to be a princess with a stepmother who is competitive for the attention of the father. The Evil Queen feels beauty is a mortal threat and what would that do to the princess herself? All kinds of flaws emerge from that."

Kitsis and Horowitz incorporated some of those themes into the writing of the show, which is why Goodwin feels the show resonates with a contemporary audience so well. "I think they've been able to flesh out these characters, ground them, and make them real and relatable without disparaging them. I feel that we still justify the original Grimm versions of these characters but we show exactly what happens off page, and off screen.

I think our objective was to make the audience feel that the impression they had of Snow White from Disney and the Brothers Grimm was an impression that was created by oral history and handed down in these stories, but the audience could see how she would be based on a real person."

The actress is also thrilled to be on a show that treats its princesses as proactive role models who aren't waiting to be saved by their male counterparts. "Yes, the women characters are so evolved and complicated," she enthuses proudly. "Their relationships are so beautiful."

She's also especially happy to be spending so much screen time with her real best friend, Jennifer Morrison, who technically plays her adult daughter,

Emma. It's a complicated conundrum to act out, considering their actual ages are only a year apart, but Goodwin says she thinks the writers really figured out how to tackle the problem in the first part of Season Two, by trapping mother and daughter in Fairy Tale Land.

"I think that the writers really took advantage of an incredible opportunity to isolate us, and to give us obstacles and conflicts that were not about our relationship and not about each other," she explains. "The obstacles were external and therefore we learned about each other navigating those obstacles and conflicts. That's how you learn the most about someone, seeing how that person handles conflict resolution. It was the opportunity we were each given. Also, it helps that we weren't given an opportunity to be self-indulgent. We weren't sitting around Mary Margaret's apartment waxing poetic and feeling sorry for ourselves about our situations. We were distracted and had to take care of each other. We had to get to know each other as women and that's really the only way to do it because these are women of the same age! Snow was a mother for a day [before the curse meant she had to send Emma away], so she doesn't have actual parenting experience. She has feelings but she isn't maternal, per se. It's something she is learning and it's great fun to learn it together."

The second half of Season Two placed Snow, Charming, Emma, Henry, and the whole Storybrooke family together for a fight against Cora and Hook, which opened up stories that Goodwin says she's excited to see unfold into the far future.

"I'm excited to learn how magic now works in this world. I'm excited for all of these characters to be together again facing what they are going to face, and learning how all the characters operate in the present. Now that we have all these conflicting memories, I love that some people wish that they didn't have the Storybrooke, Maine experience. Some characters wish they could erase their fairy tale memories and just be their Storybrooke self, yet they have to learn how to be these new amalgams of these new people." 🌸

LONG BEFORE A COMPLETED EPISODE OF *ONCE UPON A TIME* ENDS UP WOWING AUDIENCES, IT FIRST HAS TO BE CRAFTED AND DEVELOPED INSIDE THE WRITERS' ROOM. IN PART ONE OF AN EXCLUSIVE ROUND TABLE, WRITERS CHRISTINE BOYLAN, ANDREW CHAMBLISS, IAN GOLDBERG, AND DAVID H. GOODMAN TALK ABOUT THE JOURNEY THAT LED THEM TO THIS FANTASTICAL LAND AND ITS SCRIPTING CHALLENGES...

# Storytellers

Words: Paul Terry

**S**tarting with the 'stories' theme of the show, what's the story behind you joining *Once*'s writing team?

**Andrew Chambliss:** I read the *Once Upon a Time* 'Pilot' script during staffing season [the time of year when shows are hiring writers], and I remember immediately falling in love with it. Fairy tale mash-ups, flashback storytelling, and a show that was hopeful at its core... I *had* to work on it. I remember calling my agent and telling him he had to get me a meeting with [*Once* creators] Adam [Horowitz] and Eddy [Kitsis], no matter what. A few weeks later I was sitting across from them for a staffing meeting – the writer's equivalent of a job interview. In the meeting, we talked about where the guys saw the show going and what I thought I could contribute. Hearing about their plans only made me want to be a part of it even more. When the show got picked up for a full series a few weeks later, I got a call with an offer to join the writing staff. I said, "Yes!" and couldn't feel luckier to be a part of *Once*.

**Christine Boylan:** I've always been a huge fan of genre writing. Seeing real life through the lens of metaphor is, for me, the best way to get to truth. Shakespeare was a genre writer, after all. *A Midsummer Night's Dream*! *The Tempest*! Beautiful stories of magic. And in TV, shows like *Buffy*,

21

*The X-Files,* and *Twin Peaks* turned me on to the possibilities of genre in a serialized story. When I heard *Once* was hiring, I jumped at the chance to write genre for such a big stage. And lucky for me, Eddy and Adam liked my work enough to ask me to join the team.

**David H. Goodman:** It's actually a complicated story. I met Eddy and Adam when we were all writers on a show called *Birds of Prey* that aired on the old WB network. It was my first staff writing job and I looked up to them. They were seasoned pros: smart, fun to talk story with, and amazing writers. Despite all our hard work, the show was cancelled after half a season – like many shows – and we all went our separate ways. They eventually landed at *Lost*, while I spent five years on a police procedural called *Without a Trace*. Then I got back into genre TV working on the first season of *Fringe*, and then a show called *The Event*. After that, I was reading pilot scripts, and came across *Once*. It was amazing – the most original pilot I had read in a long time, so I called my agent to get a meeting. I had a leg up, I guess, because I'd worked with them before. After we met, they showed me the pilot, which blew me away. I basically just begged them to hire me and thankfully they listened!

**Ian Goldberg:** I had been a fan of Eddy and Adam's for a long time, from their work on *Lost* and *Tron: Legacy*. I used to see them around the lot at Disney all the time, back when I was working on other shows, and for some reason, I just always had this feeling or hope that we'd find a way to work together some day. When I read the pilot script for *Once*, I called up my agents and told them I would do anything to be part of the show – if they didn't need

a writer, I'd wash dishes. The script was just *that* good. When I had my interview with them, we talked about everything from fairy tales to our shared love of Woody Allen and the Coen Brothers, which is to say, we clicked.

**Of your previous writing gigs, which experiences have helped and influenced your writing on *Once*?**
**CB:** My first staff writing job was for TNT's *Leverage*, which was another kind of genre – pulpy heists and cons every week. After that I worked on *Off the Map*, a wonderful "Doctors Without Borders-in-paradise" type show for ABC. I love medical stories. And then I was at *Castle* – a good, old-fashioned mystery show. I'd also been doing some stage plays and comic books, which were fantastical in scope, but grounded in character. All of these experiences have been useful on *Once* – the con and heist research especially helped with Emma's background in Season Two's 'Tallahassee.'"
**DHG:** This might sound odd, considering it was a police procedural, but my writing on *Without a Trace* probably helped the most. Not just because I spent the most time on that show, but because every episode would delve into the life of one missing person and tell a highly emotional story about them through flashback. Obviously on *Once*, we do something similar. However, it's nice to be able to mix in dragons and magic. That beats pulling a set of fingerprints off a dead body any day.
**IG:** I think working on other 'big idea,' mythology-driven shows like *Terminator: The Sarah Connor Chronicles* and *FlashForward* was an amazing training ground. The great thing about both of those other shows is that they fostered

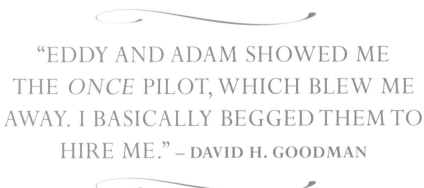

"EDDY AND ADAM SHOWED ME THE *ONCE* PILOT, WHICH BLEW ME AWAY. I BASICALLY BEGGED THEM TO HIRE ME." – DAVID H. GOODMAN

an environment where, as a writer, I felt free to pitch anything, no matter how crazy or off-the-wall an idea seemed. I was encouraged to be bold and imaginative and take big swings, which, when you think about it, is what *Once* is all about. Also, on *Terminator* in particular, we were taking established iconic characters like John and Sarah Connor and redefining them in a new context, showing the audience an entirely different side of characters they thought they knew inside and out. Imagine how excited I was when I got to apply the same kind of thinking to Snow White, Prince Charming, Rumplestiltskin, and an entire world of fairy tale characters!

**AC:** Working for Joss Whedon on *Dollhouse* has definitely influenced my writing on *Once*. The first question Joss would always ask is, "Why are we telling this story?" Basically, Joss always wanted to know if there was a reason for telling it beyond what it did for the plot. "Is there an emotional reason for telling it? Is there a thematic reason? Does it mean anything to the characters? To the audience watching at home?" If there wasn't a good answer to those questions, then we'd move onto a different story until we found one that did answer them. Eddy and Adam approach

storytelling in the same way. Sure, *Once* is about cool mash-ups, fun and inventive ways to retell stories we grew up with, but at the end of the day, it's about the characters and their emotional lives.

**What did you find was the biggest challenge in writing your first *Once* episodes?**

**CB:** I was only an avid viewer for the first season, as I joined the team right at the start of Season Two. But writers watch TV like writers – we can't help it – and I did marvel at how the writing team was able to keep the non-linear flashback stories moving along so seamlessly. That practice of creating tension, and then relieving it just enough before building it up again… that's tricky. And to accomplish it in two worlds! I think they did it so very well in Season One.

**DHG:** The biggest challenge for us on *Once*, like on any first-year show, is just finding the show. We were helped immensely by the fact that Eddy and Adam had a very strong vision for what it should be. However, even with that, there were a lot of decisions that had to be made, some through trial and error. Like, how much of the show would be in Fairy

23

Tale Land (in flashback) and how much would be in present day in Storybrooke. In some early episodes, we tried to draw too many parallels between the stories, to the point where they almost seemed like Xerox copies of one another. Then we realized that the show worked best when the flashback stories informed the present stories, instead of mirroring them.

**AC:** In FTL (Fairy Tale Land), the stories always had life-and-death stakes, involving magic, mythological creatures and the like, but in Storybrooke, the stakes were much more grounded and often revolved around characters' relationships. The key (and overall challenge) to making these two different worlds speak to each other was always making sure that the emotional stakes in Storybrooke matched the larger-than-life stakes in FTL. For instance, in 'Heart of Darkness,' we told a story about Charming desperately fighting to save Snow from killing the Queen and blackening her heart. These were pretty big stakes that involved a magical arrow and an assassination attempt. It seemed like that would be hard to match in Storybrooke, where we were telling a story about Mary Margaret trying to convince Emma and David that she had nothing to do with Kathryn's disappearance.

But, instead of trying to amp up that mystery, we focused on Mary Margaret's emotional story with David. When David doubted Mary Margaret's innocence, that moment was just as powerful as the moment where Charming jumped in front of Snow's arrow in FTL.

**IG:** In addition, I think the biggest challenge we faced was defining what the series was going to look like on a weekly basis. On a show like *Once* that's so rich with imagination and big ideas, you're constantly trying to maintain a delicate balance between stories that advance the overall mythology and more self-contained episodes that allow you to explore chapters in characters' stories in a more... well, self-contained way. *Lost* did this incredibly well, so we were very fortunate to have Eddy and Adam – who spent six years writing on that show – guiding us.

**Which fairy tale characters have you enjoyed putting the *Once* spin on the most so far, and why?**

**IG:** Anytime we get the chance to mash-up characters from one fairy tale world to another is incredibly exciting. One example that stands out for me is how we reimagined the story of Sidney, the Magic Mirror. As kids, we all grew up knowing the

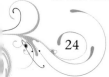

mirror as that disembodied voice on the wall in the Evil Queen's palace. But who was the person behind that voice? How did he wind up in the mirror? As we started to play around with these questions, a story took shape. What if the mirror was originally the Genie of Agrabah (from *Aladdin*)? What if he was once hopelessly in love with Regina/the Evil Queen? And what if it was this doomed love affair that ultimately drove the Genie into his trapped existence as the Mirror? Thus, we had an episode, 'Fruit of the Poisonous Tree,' which I was lucky enough to co-write with Andrew [Chambliss].

**AC:** I really loved getting to spin Snow and Charming's back-story, maybe because they're such iconic characters. We got to fill in the blanks and make them new and different while still holding onto the parts of them that are so familiar. Mashing up *The Prince and the Pauper* with Charming's origin story was so much fun because we got to explain the one thing we take for granted with Prince Charming's character –

that he's a prince. Likewise, we got to show that Snow's a more complex character than we ever thought. Not only did we get to show Snow's strong side, but we got to take her to a dark place. Who wouldn't want to write a scene where Snow White tries to hit a bluebird with her broom, only to be followed by an intervention led by Jiminy Cricket and the Seven Dwarfs?

**DHG:** I think I will always be fond of the Hook episode 'The Crocodile,' which I wrote with Robby Hull, because of the incredible reaction we got to it. We lucked out in casting Colin [O'Donoghue] as Hook. Also, and I can't take full credit for this, but the mash-up quality of the Cinderella story 'The Price of Gold,' makes it one of my favorites. When Rumplestiltskin vaporized Cinderella's Fairy Godmother, it was awesome! It was one of the early examples of how effective it was when we introduced a character you didn't expect into a story you thought you knew. That was a lesson we learned a lot from, and that led to some other great mash-ups.

"GETTING THE CHANCE TO MASH-UP CHARACTERS FROM ONE FAIRY TALE WORLD TO ANOTHER IS INCREDIBLY EXCITING." – IAN GOLDBERG

CB: Yes, I'm very pleased with what we've done so far with Captain Hook. He's funny and roguish, but there's a deep core of humanity there, of love and loss.

**What has felt different about crafting Season Two so far?**

IG: The first season ended with two massive game changers: Emma breaking the curse and Mr. Gold bringing magic to Storybrooke. So when we sat down to start coming up with stories for Season Two, it was a little bit of a, "We're not in Kansas anymore" feeling. Our characters have their memories back now... What does that mean for them? Where does Emma fit in now that she's fulfilled her duty as Savior? What exactly is Mr. Gold's agenda? Or Regina's? There are so many new, exciting elements at play right from the get-go in Season Two that it's really taking the series in unexpected and awesome directions. On top of that, we decided to expand the show by exploring new realms, including present day Fairy Tale Land which has led to us meeting people like Mulan, Sleeping Beauty, Lancelot, and Captain Hook, to name just a few.

CB: Yes, the curse is broken! All bets are off. When I first met with Eddy and Adam about joining the staff for Season Two, they pitched out the Season One finale, and I was gobsmacked. It was such a bold move – and it's just opened up the world of the show so much for Season Two. Now that these characters know who they are, there are new lands to discover, new (and old) enemies to fight, and the addition of magic to Storybrooke has empowered the good, the bad, and the neutral among our characters.

AC: Dangerous creatures, like the Wraith in the premiere, can now appear in Storybrooke just like they did last season in FTL. Ruby now has to worry about wolfing-out when the next Wolfstime approaches. Who knows how else magic will endanger the town? Plus, the real fun with this new dynamic is that we're now seeing all these FTL trappings directly [go] up against the real world. The other big difference in Season Two is that we've sent Emma and Snow back to FTL, so we're now following three different story threads instead of the two we followed in season one. We've got our

# "THE ADDITION OF MAGIC TO STORYBROOKE HAS EMPOWERED THE GOOD, THE BAD, AND THE NEUTRAL CHARACTERS."

## – CHRISTINE BOYLAN

Storybrooke story, our FTL present story, and our FTL flashback story. It can be tricky to balance all three, as Ian [Goldberg] and I found when we were writing 'Lady of the Lake,' but it's also fun to find new ways to weave three story threads together.

**DHG:** It feels like we all know the show and the characters a little better now, which makes it easier. But it's also harder, because we've told the more obvious stories and now have to dig deeper and find the things people won't expect. We've done Snow White and Cinderella, etc, but what are the stories you haven't thought of? That's a challenge.

**What are you looking forward to developing the most as Season Two progresses?**

**AC:** Emma's family. Last season, Emma – a woman who grew up never knowing her family – was fighting for the chance to become a mother to Henry. It was her shot at finally having some kind of family. It took her all season, but she finally built a relationship with Henry and saw him as her son, and this maternal love ended up breaking the Curse. What Emma wasn't expecting was that breaking the Curse would also reunite her with her parents. It's not going to be easy for Emma, Henry, Mary Margaret, or David. Emma still has feelings of resentment over being sent through the wardrobe. Mary Margaret and David missed out on their daughter's childhood. Emma's near the same age as her parents. Not to mention Regina who's making a real effort to be a good person so she can continue to be a parent to Henry, too. It's this kind of delicious messiness that's going to make building the family dynamic between these characters so much fun.

**CB:** Oh yes... Emma's journey is about to get way more complicated! I'm looking forward to seeing that story through the next few twists and turns. Mr. Gold is on a very long quest to find his son – if he does find Baelfire, what kind of reunion will it be? These are stories full of magic, set against huge backdrops, but they're just intimate, human stories.

**DHG:** One thing that made Season One so challenging, and also so great, was the way the characters didn't know who they really were. So it's been nice in Season Two to explore stories where the characters remember the histories they have with one another in Fairy Tale Land, as well as in Storybrooke. The more history these characters share, the richer their stories and emotional relationships become. They know who they love and they know who they hate. They're in on what's happening, the happiness and the heartbreak, just as much as we are.

**IG:** I'm really excited to explore the new, post-Curse Storybrooke and how that's going to change the characters we met in Season One. I'm also really looking forward to expanding our roster of Fairy Tale characters and exploring new realms like present day Fairy Tale Land, and a curiously familiar town where a renowned doctor resides, and where things always appear to be in black and white...

# Into A Swan

WHEN THE SON SHE GAVE UP FOR ADOPTION 10 YEARS PRIOR TURNED UP ON HER DOORSTEP, FORMER JAILBIRD EMMA SWAN THOUGHT LIFE COULDN'T GET ANY MORE COMPLICATED. BUT THEN SHE FOUND HERSELF IN STORYBROOKE! ACTRESS JENNIFER MORRISON TALKS ABOUT HER ROLE AS ONE OF *ONCE UPON A TIME*'S MOST PIVOTAL AND COMPLEX CHARACTERS...

Words: Tara Bennett

On the page, what seems scarier? Battling a cranky, belittling doctor for years as a hard-working, idealistic resident, or taking out crooks as a bail bondswoman, with the occasional standoffs against giants, dragons, and trolls? Actress Jennifer Morrison has done both, and can attest there's a lot more opportunity in Storybrooke and Fairy Tale Land to be the rump-kicker. Who could resist that?

Certainly not Morrison, who starred for more than five seasons on *House* as Dr. Allison Cameron, one of many to lock horns with Hugh Laurie's titular character. The actress also had a recent pivotal story arc on *How I Met Your Mother*, a role as a struggling wife and mother alongside Joel Edgerton and Tom Hardy in the Academy Award-nominated *Warrior*, and even played James T. Kirk's mom, Winona, in J.J. Abrams' *Star Trek*. When *Once Upon a Time* landed on her desk in 2011, however, she didn't look back.

"I was very lucky on *House* because as much as there were procedural elements, there was enough character development that it was still really gratifying as an actor to be a part of, and that made it worthwhile," reveals Morrison. "I did know after that I could never do a procedural, but there are so few [shows] that are serialized which last. But when I read *Once Upon a Time*, the script was absolutely extraordinary. I had never read anything like it. I thought it was so wonderful, and Emma Swan just jumped off the page. I was excited to be a part of such great material. It's one of those things in the business when a great character and great material comes along. You just say yes."

Emma Swan represented the kind of flawed yet independent persona that Morrison wanted to explore. Orphaned, initially emotionally closed-off, yet intelligent and empathetic, Swan certainly had layers. Luckily, the actress says she was looking for a character to play that had room to grow "and was going to present challenges to me over a long period of time, if it were to go over a long period of time."

In her initial chats with the show's co-creators Eddy Kitsis and Adam Horowitz, Morrison says it was clear that, "they created a very full, deep, complicated woman right from the get-go. When you have that foundation and also the comfort of hearing the way Eddy and Adam described future episodes and future seasons, I really felt confident that I was taking on something where I would be challenged and have her evolve, change, and continue to move forward in the storytelling."

## "THE SCRIPT WAS ABSOLUTELY EXTRAORDINARY. I HAD NEVER READ ANYTHING LIKE IT. I THOUGHT IT WAS SO WONDERFUL, AND EMMA SWAN JUST JUMPED OFF THE PAGE."

In Season One, Swan meets Henry, the child she gave up for adoption, and returns him to his home in Storybrooke, Maine. It's there that Henry, the enchanted town and all its mysteries envelop her life. She bonds with her son, unknowingly comes to meet her parents, Mary Margaret and David Nolan (aka Snow White and Prince Charming) and starts on the journey to fulfilling her long-delayed destiny.

Morrison says the linchpin in Season One was really having Emma's heart thaw towards Henry. "Eddy and Adam and I had a lot of talks about how Emma couldn't leave once she got to Storybrooke because she realized Henry wasn't happy," the actress shares. "The only reason she was able to live with the decision of giving him up is because she had convinced herself she had done the best thing for him, and she had really given him a better life. She had him when she was in prison! She can't imagine there would ever be a situation worse than raising a child in prison. When she realizes she didn't give him his best life, there is no way she is going anywhere until she makes sure he has a good life: whether it's with her or with someone else. Initially, it wasn't about having Henry back, but about living with the decision she made. Of course the more time she's there and spends time with Henry the more connected she becomes to him and the more she does start to feel like his mother. She develops that relationship with him and it's become more and more about being his mother than just what is best for him."

The series has also created one of the most complex mother/daughter relationships ever with the Storybrooke curse making Emma and Mary Margaret near the same age when they come together for the first time in 28 years. It begs the question of Morrison about how she approached playing that dynamic.

"There are a lot of magical coincidences that make that all work for us," Morrison explains as she laughs lightly about the weirdness of the situation. "Ginny [Goodwin] and I have been friends for years. A part of the appeal of the show was to work with her. I just saw a quote the other day that made me feel really good, where she said that when they came to

her and said they were thinking of hiring Jennifer Morrison to play Emma, she said there's no one else in the world she'd rather be stuck in another country with. I thought that was awesome because I feel the same way. You hear stories about how actors can be tricky and selfish, but that just doesn't go on with us at all. We genuinely love and care about each other. She is a generous, loving soul, so that makes it easier when you already have a friendship and chemistry.

"But I also feel like it has so much to do with the writing," Morrison continues. "Eddy and Adam did such an amazing job setting up [the fact] that Emma was everyone's caretaker in Season One because of the curse. It gave her the chance to be the caretaker, but then it shifts because she discovers this person is really her mother so she has to deal with her resentment, anger, and pain from when she was abandoned. But [in Season One] she had time to get to know Mary Margaret and realized she is a good person. So as much as she has to deal with her feelings, she can't hold it against her forever. All of that allows for the transition for accepting why she was given up, and why [her parents] had this bigger issue to be concerned about. The writing really

sets it up so that it's possible for all of those shifts to happen between them.

"Lastly, I have always felt like Emma is an overgrown teenager," she adds. "She's stunted emotionally because of what she's been through. She's never had a family unit. She doesn't know how to eat properly or take care of herself properly, but she has these incredible street smarts because she's had to survive terrible situations. It's made her an overgrown teenager. Whenever I don't know what to do with Emma, I think what would a 14-year-old boy do?" Morrison laughs. "So that also sets it up for Ginny to play

my mother, even if she's my own age, because she's coming from a place of having a very different life, different memories, and more adult decision making. Emma has always been about how I survive in this moment, which is more of that high school teenager mentality. It leaves room for there to be things for Emma to learn from Mary Margaret and things for Mary Margaret to learn from Emma because they have had such different lives."

After breaking the curse at the end of Season One, Morrison and co-star Ginnifer Goodwin (Snow) essentially spent half the second season on their

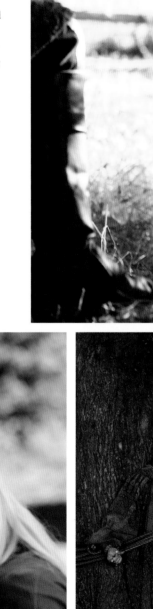

"I HAVE ALWAYS FELT LIKE EMMA IS AN OVERGROWN TEENAGER. WHENEVER I DON'T KNOW WHAT TO DO WITH HER, I THINK WHAT WOULD A 14-YEAR-OLD BOY DO?"

own new adventure when they were banished to Fairy Tale Land together. With Mulan (Jamie Chung) and Princess Aurora (Sarah Bolger) as their "road trip" companions, the four women traveled the land in their journey back to Storybrooke.

Of the arc, Morrison enthuses, "I've had a great time, and part of what made it so easy was that Sarah Bolger and Jamie Chung are just lovely girls. They immediately felt like part of the family. The four of us had a lot of fun running around the forest for months. And obviously, everything is new for Emma all over again, much like last year. Everything in Fairy Tale Land is new and she's dealing with new levels of being vulnerable and emotional in her relationship with her mom. It's exciting to be able to explore those

things, because if I stayed strong and tough with the hard-as-nails exterior, I wouldn't have been as excited, and I don't think the audience would have been either. We are actually getting to witness Emma's growth and there's nothing better than that."

This season, audiences also got to see the story of Henry's father Neal Cassidy and Emma's origins as a thief. Unlucky in love with Neal and following her brief-but-doomed connection with Sheriff Graham (Jaime Dornan), one wonders if Emma is destined for the kind of love her parents have, especially in light of her inherent powers, which were revealed to Cora (Barbara Hershey) in the midseason finale.

Morrison thinks so. "I think, ultimately, she is the product of true love, so genetically her makeup is going to want to find her own true love. What I've tried to maintain within her is that there is always this flame of hope, even if it's the tiniest flame. Even though she is so guarded and protected, there is this little flame, and you see glimpses of it at times with the Sheriff and with Hook

"I THINK, ULTIMATELY, EMMA IS THE PRODUCT OF TRUE LOVE, SO GENETICALLY HER MAKEUP IS GOING TO WANT TO FIND HER OWN TRUE LOVE."

(Colin O'Donoghue). In the flashback episode, he reminds her of herself and she sees a lot of her own pain and loss in him. Inevitably, there is a draw to that. I feel like the first season was really about Emma falling in love with Henry, knowing him and accepting that he is better off in her life. The second season has been about reconciling with her mother and father, and figuring out what it means to have parents. I think that is a stepping stone towards being capable of having love in her life. Until she worked out some of those issues, she wouldn't be able to accept love in her life in a romantic way. I think working out the family stuff is starting to put her on track to have the potential to love someone. I think it's still going to be a bumpy ride and a complicated journey for her, but I do believe that little flame of hope is always in her."

Now back in Storybrooke with Hook and Cora coming for them all, Morrison jokes that she is looking forward to not always being in a rainy forest. She adds, "It's also a little bittersweet, because I really enjoyed Sarah and Jaime, and there was a little bit of saying goodbye to two new friends. It's not going to be the four of us in the forest again. But I am excited to get everyone back into the same story. We've had so many different stories going for so long, it's nice we're all coming together. It's also finding out what that means [going forward]. What does it mean that magic is in reality? What does it mean that Henry now has two moms? So getting back to that story is exciting for me."

Us too! ✤

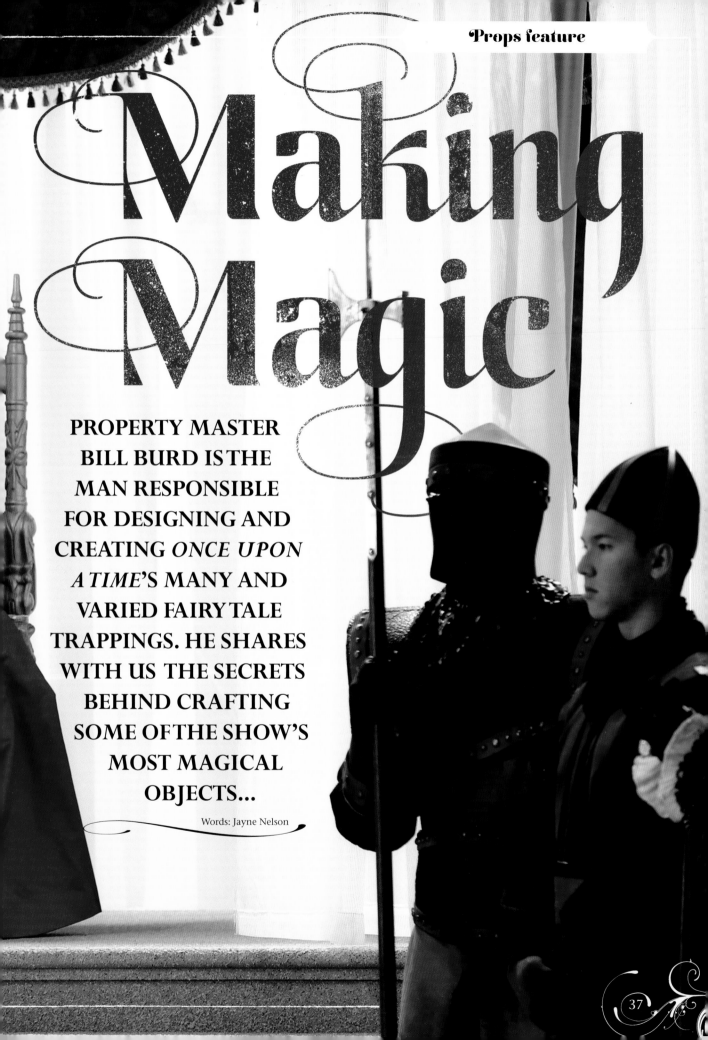

# Making Magic

**PROPERTY MASTER BILL BURD IS THE MAN RESPONSIBLE FOR DESIGNING AND CREATING *ONCE UPON A TIME*'S MANY AND VARIED FAIRY TALE TRAPPINGS. HE SHARES WITH US THE SECRETS BEHIND CRAFTING SOME OF THE SHOW'S MOST MAGICAL OBJECTS...**

Words: Jayne Nelson

There's no doubt about it: Bill Burd is a man who really loves his job as property master on *Once Upon a Time*. "From a props perspective, I think it's the juiciest plum on the tree!" he says. "I feel really fortunate. I pinch myself all the time!"

It's tough work providing props for a fairy tale-themed show, however, as Burd and his team often have to create items from scratch since they're one-of-a-kind objects that you can't just go out and buy. "There is no Medieval Big Box Store," he laughs. "Because of this need to be able to make so many different things, the department employs all sorts of specialist craftspeople including blacksmiths, leather workers, sculptors, painters, finishers, mould-makers, and jewellers.

"A props department is really a Jack of all trades," Burd explains. "There are these wonderful artisans out there struggling to find work. And a show like this keeps that whole tradition alive. I love being able to bring work to people, and benefit from their skill and their knowledge and their talent. I was at a farmer's market a little while ago and I saw a young guy standing beside a booth, about 120lbs, the last kind of person you'd think would be a blacksmith, with a table full of all these items he'd forged himself. And I've had him working on props for the show since!

"We've got a guy in our paint department too, Norm Spence, who is incredible. Anything he puts his hand to, he just transforms. You can bring him anything and when you get it back, you can't believe the work that he does. An example is when Rumplestiltskin and Hook have a sword fight. He drops a rusted old sword in front of Rumple. I gave Norm an aluminium blade in the shape of a sword, and when I got it back there were layers of rust on it and when it hit the ground, flakes rusted off... it was just fantastic!"

Another favorite of Burd's is Snow White's ring. "I love that ring! I think it's just fantastic. What I like about it is that Snow and Charming are royalty, both of them, and the ring that they have that symbolises their love is just a simple,

elegant, timeless ring and it's not an oversized rock; there's a beautiful small, green peridot set in a silver band. Peridot is an old stone, and the close-ups look great. It captures the light beautifully. I think it's a perfect symbol of their love.

"The guy who made it for me is just one of the most incredible jewellers. He did a wonderful job. His name is Sid Bianco from Goldbrite Jewellers, and he's a 70-year-old fella who is, I think, the best jeweller on the planet and I'm so glad we used him. And *he's* so glad that he had an opportunity to make Snow White and Prince Charming's wedding ring!"

Within his department itself, Burd is in charge of a team of five people who have their work cut out to create the items needed in each script. "Each of these episodes is only seven or eight days, so from the time we get the script, the clock is ticking," Burd reveals. Thankfully his department always come through in the end. "I'm fortunate to have an incredible prop team working with me," he says. "These guys all love their jobs and they're great at it. No man's an island in the film industry! This is a busy show, so none of us are sitting around. But it's a great show, a fun show, and we love working on it."

Let's take a look at some of their most memorable items...

# Weapons

"I hate to give you the standard answer that everybody expects from a props guy, but I have to say the medieval weapons are my favorite items. They're interesting for a lot of reasons other than for their purpose. If you follow the development of these weapons, it all comes from the tradespeople who are working on them. There are leather-makers and blacksmiths and woodworkers – even jewellers. As you watch the progression of science or technology, you see the changes in the weapons. It gives you a perspective of looking at a timeline of our history. I find it fascinating. That's the part of my job that I love the most – research.

"Mulan's sword, for example, has an oriental background, but we also had to do some adaptations to it to fit her character, to fit her storyline, and those adaptations had to come from the research that we do. I enjoy that a lot."

# Rumplestiltskin's Knife

"Rumplestiltskin's knife [has] its origins in Indonesian knives – they were ritualistic knives. So the design of Rumplestiltskin's knife was a real treat to work on. A funny little story about his knife: While it was getting made, it was really a laborious process. One of our machinists was working on it and I just happened to notice that Rumplestiltskin's name was misspelled! So we had to scramble to get it spelled right and make another one!"

# The Mad Hatter's Hat

"I never would have guessed that this would be the most challenging prop I've done. But it was fun! They don't make top hats any longer, and it required a milliner who knew how to put it together. We have a great milliner in our costumes department, Mitchell MacKay. He helped me out by putting me in touch with a young lady by the name of Kelly Dunlap, also known as The Saucy Milliner. She was a lot of fun to work with!

"All the fabric for the hat had to be imported, as nothing was available here. And finding a hat-block was a real challenge. Our hat is narrower at the opening than it is at the top, so when you build a hat you find a hat-block in the shape that you want, and then you either stretch or steam or starch or sew the material around it and pull the hat-block out. But because it was narrower at the bottom than it was at the top, it was a special hat-block. It was built in pieces, like a puzzle, and you put it together; you put your fabric around it and then you can pull your individual pieces out from the opening to get the hat-block out. So it was a real challenge trying to find the right hat-block for it.

"But we did, and Kelly made about a dozen hats in record time and they all looked fantastic. But about two days before we were about to go to camera with the hat, I found out that the actor [Sebastian Stan] was going to be wearing a wig, which made his hat size about two inches bigger than we'd made them! So there was a scramble to create a couple more hats that fit his head with the wig on it.

"We needed so many of the hats because some were being jumped on, some were being thrown into a fire, some were being spun to open up the portals – it was an important prop. We built 12 [at first], and we had to build another eight. We just keep going through them."

# The Genie's Lamp

"Creating the lamp was not an easy task. The most challenging aspect was the three jewels on the top of it. Originally as you made a wish, a jewel would light up, but when you finished it would go out and turn a different color. There were all these different sequences where the jewels had to light up; we needed to create a specific circuit board for it, build it inside the lab and operate it remotely with a remote control. So there was a lot to it!

"My biggest concern was that there was a scene where the lamp got thrown to the ground. I was worried it was going to shatter, or one of the jewels would pop out on camera. We made six in total and one of them was made with controls for the lights on the off-camera side, for the actor to operate, because the remote control wouldn't reach very far."

# The Hearts and Caskets

"The hearts themselves were built by our special effects make-up department and we really didn't get too involved in that, other than the caskets that they came in. We made them out of brass and copper; there's a great company up here in Vancouver that made them for us. They all look like beautifully hammered antiques."

# Hook's Hook

"I love that hook! To me a prop has to do a lot of things. It has to promote a character, promote his intentions, give you some idea of his character and background, and I thought that the hook – as simple a prop as it is – did just that. He got it from his pirate ship; it was a cargo hook. When Rumplestiltskin chopped off his hand the hook could have been a rusty, heavy piece of metal, but that just wouldn't fit Hook's character. It's highly polished, it's delicate, it looks like a surgical instrument. It's deadly."

# The Chipped Teacup

"That was an interesting prop. We scoured the town for the right-looking teacup and then we cast it in a hard-impact plastic. The retail teacups that we found, we all took turns breaking one to try and get the perfect break. We finally got it and cast that, so the break in the high-impact plastic teacup was already built into it. The other added little item was the blue painted embellishment on the cup."

# Regina's Apple Tree

"There's a crossover there between the prop department, the set decoration department, the greens department, and the construction department, because a lot of [the tree] was built. The 'hero' poison apple was made by props. We saw the apple in various forms: a pristine red juicy apple, then in another episode it's this black, kind of putrid thing that oozes black oil – that was a fun prop to build! So a simple apple had lots of different personalities that we had to give it."

# The Spellbook

"The spellbook was a really interesting build. It was designed by our production designer Michael Joy, and we had it built by an incredible book-binding company up here [in Vancouver]. The spellbook had to have a certain feel to it, an otherworldly feel, and I think Michael captured that perfectly."

# Maleficent's Staff

"I think maybe one of the most expensive single items [props which aren't duplicated, as the show often makes more than one version of a prop] would have been Maleficent's magic staff, with the dragon and the ball on it. People at Peter Charron's prop shop, Charron Studios, carved the dragon and cast that ball with the beautiful explosion of colors inside it – it took them dozens of tries to get that look inside the glass ball. Then we had to have breakaways of it and hollow ones.

"The wood that I got for that – I found a fellow on the East coast of the United States who makes his living scouring the forests for interestingly shaped strands of wood or branches. He had a collection in his warehouse of all these beautifully twisted branches and saplings – twisted naturally, by nature, into spirals. I purchased a couple from him and we skinned it and painted it and put our dragon and the ball on top of it. I thought it was quite magical."

# The Once Upon a Time Storybook

"Well, first of all I think that out of all the props that we have, the storybook is without question the most important. It carries a lot of responsibility. It may not be the most elaborate of props, but it carries the most weight. Adam and Eddy, our creators, had a lot of expectations for it, and it was a big challenge, but by the end of it everybody was happy.

"We started out by bringing in every style and type of book that we could get our hands on – from antiques to wooden covers, leather covers, cloth covers in every size... One of my guys had brought in a bunch of boxes of books from an old bookstore and in one of them was an old, linen-covered antique accounting ledger. I'm standing there with my prop guys looking at it, and I had a sense that this thing had some character to it. So we aged it up a little bit, to show to our producers and directors and the rest. It had the right size television aspect ratio – that was one of the concerns. We got everybody on site and they gave it a nod and then our art department started creating these stamps that they would press into the cover of the book.

"I went back to the book builder and brought that accounting book and some antique paper, and they made replicas of the book in the same kind of linen – it was a 1920s, early 20th-century style of book; frayed edges, that kind of thing. They put it together and stamped in the name and the designs along the edges. We created a bunch of pages with text on them, and got some artwork and put the illustrations in it, and everybody loved it!

"One of the interesting things about the book is that we do a lot of transitions from the book and into live-action. Often if we're fortunate enough to have the live action scheduled first in our shooting order, then we can take a screengrab of that and create an illustration from the screengrab and insert it into the book. But if our schedule is before the action part of the storyline, then we put a green page in there and our VFX dept will screengrab the live action later on and turn it into an illustration."

# it's good to be bad

RUTHLESS, SCHEMING, AND ALWAYS
SHARPLY DRESSED, REGINA CUTS A SCARY FIGURE,
WHETHER AS THE EVIL QUEEN OF FAIRY TALE LAND,
OR THE CONTROLLING MAYOR OF STORYBROOKE.
HOWEVER, THERE IS VULNERABILITY BEHIND THE
VILLAINY. LANA PARRILLA TALKS ABOUT PLAYING
THE QUEEN WHO HIDES HER HURT
WITH HEARTLESSNESS…

Words: Tara Bennett

Regina Mills (aka the Evil Queen) should really be the woman we all just hate. After all, her vengeful actions as the Mayor of Storybrooke, or as the venial, dark magic-conjuring queen in Fairy Tale Land have done little to endear her to… well, anyone. Yet as the layers of the proverbial Regina onion have been peeled away over a season and a half on *Once Upon a Time*, she's actually starting to earn some of our compassion as we've learned of the tragic love and loss that's shaped her gnarled path.

That we can see any worth to the woman at all is in great measure due to the nuance that actress Lana Parrilla brings to her portrayal of Regina and the Queen. But

that's par for the course for Parrilla, who has a habit of getting cast on shows (*Boomtown*, *24*, *Swingtown*) and quickly turning her characters into standouts. And it's what she's done with the deliciously devilish, dual role on *Once Upon a Time*, embracing the dark side of Regina/the Evil Queen, yet always tempering her ruthless ways with grounding pathos.

"When I put the costumes on it's like an instant transformation, but you also feel really powerful," Parrilla shares with us about becoming the Evil Queen. "If you look in the mirror, it's so crazy. There's no semblance of who I am. I can't even see my face anymore, because everything is lighter, and the hair and the costume. You feel like an action hero. I do! I feel kind of heroic when I put them on."

And that's despite the fact that her character is often doing far from heroic things. But even with her penchant to do bad, from her first read of the *Once Upon a Time* 'Pilot' script Parrilla says she never saw Regina as a one-note villain. There's been confirmation of that fact with each subsequent script reveal, from her lover Daniel's tragic death to her mother Cora's despicable machinations; all of the context has made Regina's slow evolution one of the most compelling arcs of the entire series.

"I absolutely love Regina and the path she is on now, which is the road to redemption," Parrilla enthuses to us about one half of her on-screen persona. "I love that she is such a complex character, and that there is nothing black or white about her. She is multi-layered and multi-colorful. I love playing her, and sometimes it's really hard. Oh God," she sighs heavily. "She truly is a tortured soul, but I have a lot of empathy for her and compassion for the character. When I think about where she comes from and the things she's experienced in her life, it's quite tragic."

As to how she compartmentalizes both versions of her character, Parrilla considers it and offers, "I was just talking to someone about playing the two characters, and sometimes they're one for me. I can't really bring the Mayor into Fairy Tale Land, but I can definitely bring the Fairy Tale Land Queen into Storybrooke. It's a lot of fun finding those moments where maybe I can say a line in the Evil Queen voice now that all the characters have merged and the Curse has been lifted."

Speaking of that Curse, Regina's almost three-decades-long spell was surprisingly dissolved at the end of Season One, which left Regina a pariah in her town and far more vulnerable than we've ever seen her. Parrilla agrees and says playing her is, "a little bit more challenging than it was the first season, because [the townspeople] are all now dealing with these memories, but the Evil Queen/Regina has always had those types of memories. I think for

her, having lived in Storybrooke for 28 years laced with those memories, there are huge regrets: the hatred, the anger, the longing for Daniel. It's really interesting that her memory wasn't erased, and I wonder if that was a curse or a blessing for her, while everyone else forgot about who they were. For example, Jiminy Cricket – he didn't really like certain things that he did back in Fairy Tale Land. I look at that and go, 'Well, was Regina doing everyone a favor?'" she laughs.

Regina and Mr. Gold are now struggling with her reliance on magic to regain control of her life, and it's proving to be a slippery slope of temptation for both of them. Parrilla muses, "There's a moment when the young Regina uses magic for the first time and Rumplestiltskin asks her how it felt? She says, 'I loved it.' She hates that she loves it, so it's the addict's

> "FOR REGINA, I THINK WHEN SHE LOVES, SHE PROBABLY LOVES DEEPER THAN MOST…"

> # "I CAN'T REALLY BRING THE MAYOR INTO FAIRY TALE LAND, BUT I CAN DEFINITELY BRING THE FAIRY TALE LAND QUEEN INTO STORYBROOKE."

mind when it comes to Regina. It's how she's manipulated things and gotten everything she wants. But then she hates it because it's a crutch. She needs that in order to get what she wants and without it, she actually does have to do the work. She has to dig deep and take a good look at herself. As tempting as magic is for her to use with the curse lifted, a part of her knows that if she does, she's doomed. She'll never grow and will lose everyone. She has no choice but to go down the magic-less path and live more like a real human being. I think there's a part of her that knows that as uncomfortable as it is to be in her body, she probably knows it's the best choice. We'll see how long that lasts," she laughs. "There's a love and hate, and an internal struggle for her."

One of the most interesting aspects of Season Two is the revelation about just how destructive a force Cora has been in Regina's life. Yet, Regina is still more interested in seeing Snow as her nemesis than her own mother.

Parrilla agrees. "I think it's been interesting how Regina has gone about plotting her revenge and getting back

she wants to be, or who she is, the love for her mother is undeniable. Whatever happens she loves her mother, so I think it was very hard for her to blame her mom. She must have a very hard time assigning responsibility to the person who is doing the wrong. She goes after Snow, and yes, she broke a promise. You may want to punish someone for that, but it's another thing to want to kill them," she laughs. "It's really hard to rationalize some of that behavior, because I'm a sane person playing an insane person. A lot of it doesn't quite connect and I like that it doesn't. It challenges me to understand what her psychology is in life. Everything is slightly elevated and she's a little off," she chuckles.

"One thing we haven't seen enough of is her relationship with her mother growing up," she adds. "We've only seen them later. I'd like to see how they got there. I'm very curious about that."

Her twisted parental relationship has certainly been carried through with her adopted son, Henry. She almost lost him forever at the end of Season One, and since then she's been struggling to do what's best for him... not her. She's getting in touch with a

## Did You Know?

The name Regina means "queen" in Latin – a sign perhaps that Cora had ambitions for her daughter to become royalty even when she first named her.

The Evil Queen in the *Snow White* story has been portrayed by a number of actresses in different adaptations over the years. As well as Lana Parrilla, she has been played by the likes of Sigourney Weaver, Dianne Wiest, Miranda Richardson, Dame Diana Rigg, Julia Roberts, and Charlize Theron, among others. In the classic Disney animated version of the story, the character was voiced by the screen and stage actress Lucille La Verne.

In the original Brothers Grimm story, the Evil Queen tries to kill Snow White by asphyxiating her using a too tightly laced corset and by giving her a poisoned comb to use, before she offers her the famous poisoned apple.

at Snow White, and how that has been her focus and not her mother. I would think she would have just blamed her mother initially, because it happened right before her eyes. So why did she then turn to Snow White? And then we go into the psychology, which is where I have to go to play the character, so I think it comes from children not ever wanting their parents to be wrong. Mom and dad are everything when you're growing up. Despite Cora not letting her be who

# "I LOVE THAT REGINA IS SUCH A COMPLEX CHARACTER, AND THAT THERE IS NOTHING BLACK OR WHITE ABOUT HER. SHE IS MULTI-LAYERED AND MULTI-COLORFUL. I LOVE PLAYING HER, AND SOMETIMES IT'S REALLY HARD."

depth of love she hasn't experienced since Daniel, and the actress says it's been fascinating to have Regina struggle through it.

"For Regina, I think when she loves, she probably loves deeper than most," the actress explains. "Let's break down Daniel and that relationship for a second. They had a love and she was very young when he was killed. She created this Curse and everything that happened was for him. She kissed that ring and said, "We got her, Daniel. We got her." The level of loyalty there... I can only assume it would have to be there for Henry as well. She wants love, to feel love, and to give love. Usually with babies it's unconditional and I feel like she wants that in her life. In having it for 10 years, I'm curious to get some flashbacks about it to see what

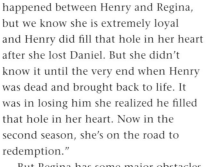

happened between Henry and Regina, but we know she is extremely loyal and Henry did fill that hole in her heart after she lost Daniel. But she didn't know it until the very end when Henry was dead and brought back to life. It was in losing him she realized he filled that hole in her heart. Now in the second season, she's on the road to redemption."

But Regina has some major obstacles to overcome still this season before she can earn that redemption… and a lot of it will come back to mother. In teasing her next major arc, Parrilla says, "Regina has anxieties and fears about her mother that haunt her in Storybrooke. She has no idea where Cora is. Just the thought of Cora ever entering her life again is terrifying for multiple reasons. One, it's just having to confront her mother after all that she's done to her. I pushed her through a mirror and sent her off to another

land! I remember when I was a kid and did something wrong, I was so terrified I'd crawl under the bed to hide. I would put things in front of me," she laughs. "My father is deceased, but if my father would walk through the doors right now – obviously I would be so happy – but if I did something wrong, even at 35 years old I would be [terrified]. You revert to the child in you when you're with your parents. If she were to see Cora, I think there's going to be all these mixed emotions. There's always love for your mom, but then there's, 'She's going to kick my ass!' Not only that, but she's going to destroy everything that we created. There's fear in that and Cora is a very powerful sorcerer. [After] 28 years of not using magic, Regina is going to have to sharpen up a bit. She's really rusty, so if Cora were to come to Storybrooke, I think they're probably going to go at it." ✜

# Dressing the Part

Words: Tara Bennett

*ONCE UPON A TIME* BRINGS WITH IT A WEALTH OF GORGEOUS COSTUMES, FROM THE EVIL QUEEN'S VILLAINOUS GLAMOR, TO MARY MARGARET'S CHIC PRETTINESS. IT'S COSTUME DESIGNER EXTRAORDINAIRE EDUARDO CASTRO WHO DREAMS UP AND PUTS TOGETHER THE CHARACTERS' WARDROBE, AND HERE HE TELLS US HOW HE DOES IT – AND TAKES US THROUGH SOME FAVORITE LOOKS…

"RED IN THE FOREST"

Once Upon A Time

Cinderella @ the Ball

BLUE SPARKLY SHEER LACE OVER TAFFETA

"Once Upon A Time"

From the lavish gowns of the Evil Queen to the distinct hats that rest on the heads of all seven dwarfs, every costuming detail and design on *Once Upon a Time* is born from the mind and sketch pad of award-winning costume designer Eduardo Castro. A four-time Costume Designers Guild Award winner for *Ugly Betty*, Castro is a 30-year costuming veteran who's got an impressive resume of varied iconic film and television credits.

"The first one I did was *Fame*," he tells us from his office in Vancouver. "It was fast and furious with musical numbers. But I think the first [show] that made the big difference for me was *Miami Vice* in 1985 and 1986. It's where I got my chops to do this kind of stuff. It threw me right into the frying pan of something I was not familiar with, which was high fashion. They sent me to Paris and Milan. What happened on *Miami Vice* was I got my feel and instinct for very expensive pieces. You can't learn that right off the bat. You have to feel it. Seeing it in magazines is one thing, but handling it day-to-day and seeing how clothes fit prepared me to do other shows like *Ugly Betty* and now *Once Upon a Time*."

Castro says he threw his hat into the ring for the costume designer position after he read the script and was intrigued by the show's ambition. "I tell you, I was approached after other designers were approached for the Pilot, and I think the key factor was that I said it was possible when the other people said it wasn't," he chuckles heartily. "I got hired over the phone – possibly because of the excitement I had about creating a new world and creating fairytales that are anchored in a tradition but still modernizing them. My very first meeting with [co-creators] Eddy Kitsis and Adam Horowtitz in LA, I opened my ideas for the first drawings and they were just so excited and on the same page."

In creating the show's wardrobe aesthetic for Storybrooke and Fairy Tale Land, Castro says he looked at basic illustrations from fairytales for inspiration. "Back when we started the Pilot the anchor was to push the envelope with making these things more modern. But as we found our way, I found that what we really needed to anchor more was in Fairy Tale Land. So there was a silhouette based on a lot of those illustrations and then in our own minds as we grow up, we have our own vision."

"Honest, this is probably the easiest thing I've ever done because it was set up in a certain way," Castro enthuses about the show. "I came up to Vancouver to do the Pilot and I thought it was going to be a misery because it can be very, very busy during pilot season. I was told everybody worth anything was unavailable or already picked up. But there was a little guardian angel on our show, and what happened was when I got up here, the new film version of *Superman* [*Man of Steel*] got delayed, so I inherited that crew. I got an incredible crew who set the show up so well and quite a few have stayed on with me. The elements were right. We only had four weeks to do the Pilot and we had 300 extras for Snow White's wedding! But all of the pieces of the puzzle fit perfectly.

I inherited an amazing workroom. Having had the experience of doing *Ugly Betty*, I know what's out in stores. I know what looks good and that helps an awful lot when we approach the modern looks.

"We were also very blessed with a very good script and producers who trusted me, which is fantastic because television can be a tough venue with a brutal approval process," Castro continues. "But with this project it was just fantastic. Everything worked out so well, like a Swiss clock. It's an unusual thing."

With a large ensemble cast, two worlds and now merged personalities for many of the characters, there's a lot to design and manage in every episode of *Once*. Overall, Castro says, "What we want to present to the audience is something that makes them go, 'Ooh!'"

Opening up his sketchbook, Castro shares with us some secrets about the designs behind many of the show's incredible looks…

**Rumplestiltskin/Mr. Gold** – "The one thing they changed throughout the Pilot, and it was changed for the better, was Rumplestiltskin's costume. Robert [Carlyle] was the first person to arrive in Vancouver and we had a nice medieval costume with an elaborate hood. The notes that came back from the creators were that, 'He's just not sexy.' Eddy Kitsis and Adam Horowitz said, 'Just think rock star,' so we found these crocodile skins, with the high boots and the tight pants. We made him an evil rock star, and that's how Rumple was born. As we've moved forward, he's always had a sexy element, even as Mr. Gold when he's in a Dolce & Gabbana suit. Again, this comes from experience – nothing fits like a Dolce suit on his small frame, and it's a martini line, which is super slim. Robert fell in love with it, and had I not had that kind of experience, it might not have happened so fast."

**Prince Charming/David** – "Here's a secret – Charming is wearing the same pants all the way through [the series]. They're just leather pants. Even more of a secret is that every member of the cast wears those pants. We realized that the leather pants had a modern edge, and they just make for a sexy silhouette. Then we add the period-looking doublets, tops or jackets that have that fairytale quality. On the Storybrooke side, for Charming this season I found an old Belstaff jacket at the ABC Costume Company. We went to great expense to duplicate it in leather, and everything about it is sexy without trying very hard. He wears the same jeans all the way through, and simple shirts."

**Snow White/Mary Margaret** – "She embodies a nobility and romance. You have to take into consideration the actor. Ginny has a body language, eyes that do things, and there's something about her that you want to go in a certain direction and put things on her. She can pull off things in the modern world that are very fashion-forward, but sexy at the same time. Like this morning we were working on a funeral sequence, dressing her in a white Alexander McQueen blouse, a Rachel Zoe skirt, and a Vivienne Westwood cloak. We want to keep her whimsical, fun, and interesting to look at. We want to avoid a very generic look.

"This season, Snow has been in the same costume for nine episodes. It's the lavender sweater and Club Monaco chemise, but we reworked her so when she comes back to Storybrooke she looks like she just came off a runway in Paris. We decided she needed to look like Audrey Hepburn in *Funny Face*. It's a fun '60s vibe. And all of a sudden she becomes more adventurous in her sensuality now."

**Emma** – "In the Pilot Emma was in a black jacket, but the day before we shot, Eddy asked if it could be red. I found a cheap jacket and overnight we tweaked it. By episode three of last season, we replaced it with my version of a custom jacket, but the fit was much better. We got in touch with the company Ocean Drive, who [in my opinion] make the best leather jackets, and Jennifer Morrison loved them! Another interesting note was about the red dress she wears on the date in the Pilot. We'd tried a Dolce dress and a Gucci dress, but we went with a $79 dress. When we photographed the expensive dresses, they didn't look [expensive]! The key to doing what we do is that sometimes these high-ticket items don't look as good [on camera]."

**The Evil Queen/Regina** – "Lana can make a $79 jacket look amazing. For example, we just found this coat from Zara and it looks like a $2,000 coat. Or we discovered that I can put a Gucci on her and on top of that I can put a cheaper jacket in a cool cranberry or dark green color.

In a recent episode, all of a sudden, things changed and we needed a new costume for the Evil Queen – and we had three days. We used a leather skirt we had already used, and a Bebe black leather jacket. We added a belt and re-cut the collar, and she wore that. The jacket had great shoulders and then when you put the gauntlets on, it all of a sudden became a very cool outfit.

What we found with Lana as Regina is that we have custom-made a lot of her pants and suits, because she likes them high-waisted and they are very hard to find. We found a Pink Tartan-designed suit and we copy it in really great fabrics."

^ Ep. 109
Hat: made by Mitchell.

Cape - embossed leather from Lonsdale.

gloves/gauntlets. - gloves from Danier. Ocean drive. purple leather was painted by Dye Dept.

lining - Fab coq.

Rokko / Cloak.

Boots: oh god. : Locale wedge platform heel.

Pants: Danier size O.

**Sleeping Beauty/Aurora** – "I think one of the most glamorous dresses we ever made was for Sleeping Beauty, but I don't think its detail translated onto the screen. The fabric was manufactured. We made it from four different fabrics cut apart and woven together. Our inspiration was [designers] Rodarte. It just didn't translate on screen because the dress had to do so many things, and we had to put a cloak on it so she wears that most of the time. Close up, that was magnificent and it took hours and hours of development."

**Red's Mother, Anita** – "It's a knockout piece and an amazing costume. She lives in the forest so it's a little organic; basically a sexy corset. She has the leather pants, boots, and a skirt that we made out of interesting fabrics. It works out quite well. She's played by Annabeth Gish and she looks very much like Red. She was excited and thrilled with it, and it's one of the most successful costumes we've done."

# Season One – the Episode

SEASON ONE NOT ONLY INTRODUCED US TO STORYBROOKE, FAIRY TALE LAND, AND MANY OF THE CHARACTERS WHO INHABIT THEM, IT ALSO INCLUDED MAGICAL DEALS AND BROKEN CURSES, POISONED APPLES AND TRUE LOVE'S KISS. JOIN US AS WE LOOK BACK OVER ALL THE EPISODES OF THE FIRST YEAR...

Words: Chad Ross

## 1.01 'Pilot'

**SNOW WHITE:** "Where are we going?"
**THE QUEEN:** "Somewhere horrible. Absolutely horrible. A place where the only happy ending will be *mine*."

**Plot:** On her birthday, bail bondswoman Emma Swan is surprised when Henry, the child she gave up for adoption 10 years before, turns up on her doorstep. Taking him home introduces her to the town of Storybrooke, Maine, which Henry claims is under a fairy tale curse, with Emma its unwitting savior. Emma meets some new friends and makes a powerful enemy, but decides to stay a while...

**Introducing:** All of our main characters, many with familiar tales. Important characters with no fairy tale antecedents (so far!) are bail bondswoman Emma Swan, and Henry Mills, the young son she gave up for adoption 10 years before. Both will be pivotal in lifting the curse that Storybrooke is under.

**Once Upon a Time...** We learn in the flashbacks to Fairy Tale Land that the Evil Queen cursed her fellow inhabitants to a land with no happy endings. Emma escaped the curse thanks to her parents Snow White and Prince Charming, and Rumplestiltskin is privy to some pretty classified information.

**Did You Notice?** Dr. Hopper whistles the tune 'Give a Little Whistle,' a song sung by Jiminy Cricket in the classic Disney animation, *Pinocchio*. When Emma wakes up in the police cell, Leroy is whistling 'Whistle While you Work' from the Disney movie *Snow White and the Seven Dwarfs*.

## 1.02 'The Thing You Love Most'

**MALEFICENT:** "Don't do this, this Curse. There are lines even we shouldn't cross. All power comes with a price. Enacting it will take a terrible toll. It will leave an emptiness inside you – a void you will never be able to fill."
**EVIL QUEEN:** "Then so be it."

**Plot:** Regina steps up her plan to run Emma out of town, but ironically this makes her more determined than ever to stay. Meanwhile, Regina realizes that Mr. Gold is responsible for Emma coming to Storybrooke, and just how deep their rivalry goes.

**Introducing:** In Fairy Tale Land we're introduced to the Evil Queen's Magic Mirror, and its Storybrooke counterpart, reporter Sidney Glass (Giancarlo Esposito). Kristin Bauer van Straten also guests as the Evil Queen's frenemy and fellow witch, Maleficent.

**Once Upon a Time...** We find out how the Evil Queen came across the Dark Curse, and the lengths to which she was prepared to go in making it work, even sacrificing her beloved father.

**Did You Notice?** Regina's apple tree in Storybrooke is the same as the one the Queen tends in Fairy Tale Land.

## 1.03 'Snow Falls'

**PRINCE CHARMING:** "Well, if you need anything..."
**SNOW WHITE:** "You'll find me."
**PRINCE CHARMING:** "Always."

**Plot:** Emma persuades Mary Margaret, at Henry's request, to read from Henry's storybook to the amnesiac 'John Doe' in the hospital who Henry is convinced is Mary Margaret's true love. To their great shock he wakes up, but with no memory of his life before. Just as it seems he and Mary Margaret are destined for one another, Regina introduces someone who will thwart their happiness. Meanwhile, Mary Margaret offers Emma a place to stay.

**Introducing:** We meet Princess Abigail (Anastasia Griffith), the seemingly spoilt princess whom Charming is engaged to in Fairy Tale Land. In Storybrooke she is Kathryn Nolan, the wife of Charming's amnesiac other self, David.

**Once Upon a Time...** We discover how Charming and Snow first met, and also something of the power of true love, both in Fairy Tale Land and in Storybrooke.

**Did You Notice?** Walter, the Storybrooke version of Sleepy, appropriately enough falls asleep and misses David escaping from the hospital.

## 1.04 'The Price of Gold'

EMMA: "What do you want?"
MR. GOLD: "Oh, I don't know just yet. You'll owe me a favor."
EMMA: "Deal."

**Plot:** Emma meets a young girl in a predicament linked to Mr. Gold, and our heroine has to make a deal to help her out of it. She also gets a job offer, one that she knows will annoy Regina, while Regina proves to be keeping a secret about who she spends her time with when no one's around.

**Introducing:** We meet Cinderella (Jessy Schram), who makes a fateful deal with Rumplestiltskin after he makes sure her Fairy Godmother meets a nasty end. In Storybrooke, she's the pregnant teenager Ashley Boyd.

**Once Upon a Time...** We discover a little more about Rumplestiltskin and his ability to persuade people to make deals with him despite his shady dealings, as well as how difficult it is to break one of his pacts. Cinderella discovers this to her cost, as she loses her husband while trying to keep her baby.

**Did You Notice?** Cinderella got her name because she lives among the cinders or ashes from the kitchen – her Storybrooke counterpart is appropriately called Ashley. Cinderella in the original German version of the fairy tale is the similar Aschenputtel.

## 1.05 'That Still Small Voice'

HENRY: "Hey, listen, they're back. Crickets. Things are changing."

**Plot:** During their therapy sessions Henry tries to convince Archie that he's really Jiminy Cricket. Meanwhile Regina threatens Archie that he must destroy Henry's "delusions." Emma begins her new job as deputy sheriff and things begin to change even more in Storybrooke. When Henry finds himself in danger, Emma and Archie put their lives on the line to save him.

**Introducing:** We meet Jiminy's nasty parents Martin (Harry Groener) and Myrna (Carolyn Hennesy), whose evil ways spur Jiminy into wanting to live a different life.

**Once Upon a Time...** We discover the back-story of Archie/Jiminy, as the son who longed to escape his criminal parents. When the Blue Fairy grants his wish, he becomes a cricket, and a conscience, who will encourage others to do the right thing.

**Did You Notice?** Dr. Hopper's pet Dalmatian, Pongo, has the same name as the father dog from the book and movies *101 Dalmatians*.

## 1.06 'The Shepherd'

DR. WHALE: "The smallest thing can trigger your memories."

**Plot:** The amnesiac David Nolan returns home to a life he doesn't remember, and tries to choose between his wife Kathryn and Mary Margaret, for whom he has strong feelings. David chooses Mary Margaret, but thanks to Regina's intervention, he is manipulated into going back to Kathryn – much to Mary Margaret's disappointment. Meanwhile, Emma discovers Regina and Sheriff Graham's secret affair.

**Introducing:** We meet King George (Alan Dale), Prince James' authoritarian father. It later turns out that his Storybrooke counterpart is District Attorney Albert Spencer.

**Once Upon a Time...** We find out more about Prince Charming's back-story, and how he was really a shepherd who was maneuvered into replacing his dead twin brother as Prince James thanks to the dealings of King George and the ever wily Rumplestiltskin.

**Did You Notice?** Emma offers Mary Margaret a measure of MacCutcheon whisky – a fictional brand featured in the series *Lost*, which *Once Upon a Time*'s co-creators Edward Kitsis and Adam Horowitz were writers/executive producers on.

# 1.07 'The Heart is a Lonely Hunter'

**GRAHAM:** "I don't feel anything, Regina... I'd rather have nothing than settle for less. Nothing is better than what we have. I need to feel something, Regina, and the only way to do that is to give myself a chance."

**Plot:** Sheriff Graham starts to remember his past life as the Huntsman in Fairy Tale Land, making him question what he's doing with Regina, and Emma wonders whether she has feelings for him. When Graham becomes convinced that his heart is missing, Emma follows him on his journey to find it, but the quest has fatal results.

**Introducing:** This episode is the first time we meet Sheriff Graham's Fairy Tale Land counterpart, the Huntsman – who was raised by wolves and chosen to hunt down Snow.

**Once Upon a Time...** The Huntsman's tragic story is revealed, showing how he lost his heart as a result of his compassion for Snow White. The Huntsman is consequently punished by the Evil Queen making sure he never feels anything again.

**Did You Notice?** Sheriff Graham's last name, Humbert, is the first name of the Huntsman in Disney's *Snow White and the Seven Dwarfs*.

# 1.08 'Desperate Souls'

**DARK ONE:** "My life was such a burden. You'll see – magic always comes with a price, and now it's yours to pay."

**Plot:** As Storybrooke recovers from the shock of Graham's death, Emma decides to run for Sheriff, but faces opposition from Regina, who puts Sidney Glass up to stand as her opponent. Emma joins forces with Mr. Gold, much to Henry's dismay, as he has second thoughts about breaking the Curse after Sheriff Graham's death. Regina and Gold resort to dirty tricks, but Emma stands for her principles. However, not all is as it seems, as deception runs deep.

**Introducing:** We're introduced to Rumplestiltskin's son Baelfire (Dylan Schmid) who disappeared during an attempt to get him and his father out of Fairy Tale Land. Mr. Gold has since spent many years trying to find him.

**Once Upon a Time...** We finally start to learn what motivates Rumplestiltskin; his love for his son and desire to protect him turned him into the dark figure he became. Ironically, in trying to protect his son he became something his son was scared of.

**Did You Notice?** The Dark One and Rumplestiltskin mention the names that the miller's daughter in the original *Rumplestiltskin* fairy tale guesses wrongly are his name.

# 1.09 'True North'

**EVIL QUEEN:** "Tell me why? Hmm. Why did your children refuse me?"
**WOODCUTTER:** "Because we're a family. And family always finds one another."

**Plot:** Emma gets involved in trying to help two runaways, Nicholas and Ava Zimmer, find their father before they're separated in foster care. And while there i no guarantee their father will want them when he finds out about them, Emma's past has given her a special insight that might prove persuasive. However, Regina is determined to throw a spanner in the works and stop her.

**Introducing:** We meet Hansel (Quinn Lord) and Gretel (Karley Scott Collins), as well as their father The Woodcutter (Nicholas Lea). Perhaps more importantly, we meet August W. Booth (Eion Bailey), the first stranger to come to Storybrooke since Emma, and someone who will prove instrumental i helping to lift the curse.

**Once Upon a Time...** The Evil Queen finds two children who have lost their father in the forest, and sees in them an opportunity to steal a powerful weapon to use against Snow. When the Evil Queen makes the children an offer afterward, she learns something of the power of family.

**Did You Notice?** The comic book Henry reads in the opening is *Ultimate Wolverine Vs. Hulk*, written by Damon Lindelof, who worked with *Once Upon a Time* co-creators Edward Kitsis and Adam Horowitz on *Lost*.

# 1.10 '7.15AM'

RUMPLESTILTSKIN: "Don't doubt yourself now, dearie. Love makes us sick. Haunts our dreams. Destroys our days. Love has killed more than any disease."

**Plot:** A suspicious Regina asks Emma to investigate the mysterious stranger who has arrived in town, because she is worried about his influence on Henry. As a storm approaches Storybrooke, Mary Margaret and David struggle with their feelings for one another, before reaching a decision.

**Introducing:** We meet Stealthy (Geoff Gustafson), one of the original eight dwarfs.

**Once Upon a Time...** Snow hears about Charming's impending marriage, and enlists some help from Rumplestiltskin to try and forget him – but a letter from Charming changes her mind. Setting out to find Charming, she's captured by King George, who threatens Charming's life. To protect him, Snow relents. Just as Charming has decided to call the wedding off and fight for Snow, it turns out she has taken drastic measures to heal her broken heart.

**Did You Notice?** When Snow meets Grumpy for the first time, he's humming 'Heigh Ho,' the dwarfs' song in *Snow White and the Seven Dwarfs*.

# 1.11 'Fruit of the Poisonous Tree'

GENIE: "Making a wish comes with a price."

**Plot:** Emma joins forces with an apparently disillusioned Sidney Glass to expose Regina's corruption, but there is more to the story than Emma realizes, and she is being played.

**Introducing:** In this episode we see for the first time King Leopold (Richard Schiff), Snow's father and Regina's husband (much to her regret).

**Once Upon a Time...** The story of the Genie who became the Magic Mirror is revealed, and his relationship with the Evil Queen was a lot closer than we might have imagined. We witness more of the Evil Queen's gift for manipulation, as she persuades the Genie to act as her cat's paw in dealing with her husband Leopold, as well as her cruelty in making the Genie her Magic Mirror so he can be with her and gaze upon her forever – an ironic twist on his stated wish.

**Did You Notice?** It's revealed in this episode that the Evil Queen's first name is Regina in Fairy Tale Land as well as Storybrooke.

# 1.12 'Skin Deep'

EVIL QUEEN: "True love's kiss will break any curse."

**Plot:** When an act of vandalism occurs on Mr. Gold's house, Emma believes he will seek vigilante justice for it. Meanwhile, a Valentine's Day girls' night is planned with Mary Margaret, Ruby, and Ashley. Regina and Gold make it clear that they know who each other really are, but Regina has an ace up her sleeve – unbeknownst to Gold she is keeping hidden one of the things Gold wants most in the world.

**Introducing:** We first meet the beautiful Belle (Emilie de Ravin), the captive who grows to become the love of Rumplestiltskin's life. As we discover, her Storybrooke counterpart has been confined in a psychiatric ward by Regina to keep her away from Mr. Gold.

**Once Upon a Time...** More of Rumplestiltskin's history is revealed, as he is shown to be the 'Beast' with whom Belle makes a deal in order to save her town, finding unexpected love for him in the process. But Rumplestiltskin is not willing to accept that he loves her more than he loves his power.

**Did You Notice?** Objects in Rumplestiltskin's castle reference the Beast's castle in Disney's *Beauty and the Beast*, including the clock, the candelabra, the teapot, and, of course, the chipped teacup.

# 1.13 'What Happened to Frederick'

**PRINCE CHARMING:** "True love isn't easy but it must be fought for, because once you find it, it can never be replaced."

**Plot:** Still trying to work out their feelings for each other, David tells Mary Margaret he chooses her over Kathryn, and breaks up with Kathryn, without telling her why. Regina interferes and shows Kathryn pictures of Mary Margaret and David together, causing Kathryn to publicly confront Mary Margaret at the school. Consequently, Mary Margaret is ostracized by the townspeople and tells David they're over. Kathryn goes missing, and Regina hides an important letter left behind by Kathryn.

**Introducing:** Princess Abigail's true love, Frederick (Greyston Holt) is introduced. His Storybrooke counterpart, teacher Jim, bumps into Abigail's counterpart Kathryn and later finds her empty car when she disappears.

**Once Upon a Time...** Abigail tells Charming she knows he doesn't love her, and that she's in love with someone else herself. She enlists his help in saving her lost love Frederick, who has been turned into a golden statue. Charming succeeds, but King George, enraged that the marriage between Charming and Abigail is off, is determined to track him down and destroy him.

**Did You Notice?** *Space Paranoids*, the video game Henry plays, is a fictional game from the Disney movie *Tron*.

# 1.14 'Dreamy'

**DREAMY:** "I believe you can do anything you want, as long as you can dream it."

**Plot:** Desperate for people to like her, Mary Margaret volunteers to help out with Miner's Day, but the townspeople still hate her. She manages to enlist the curmudgeonly Leroy, however, who is smitten with the klutzy nun Astrid and wants to help her and her sisters from being evicted by Mr. Gold. Somehow, with a little trickery on Leroy's part, they succeed.

**Introducing:** The fairy Nova (Amy Acker) makes her debut, and soon attracts the attention of Dreamy/Grumpy (Lee Arenberg). Dreamy's Storybrooke counterpart Leroy is similarly smitten with Astrid, her Storybrooke identity, though inconveniently for him, she's a nun in this land!

**Once Upon a Time...** The back-story of Grumpy is revealed – dwarf Dreamy falls for the fairy Nova, but though they have big dreams of a life together, their respective leaders – Bossy and the Blue Fairy – keep them apart. Their dreams dashed, Dreamy becomes Grumpy.

**Did You Notice?** When Mary Margaret and Leroy are selling candles door to door, they come across a skinny man who's eating a carrot, and a fat lady is sitting with him. This is a nod to Jack Sprat and his wife from the nursery rhyme.

# 1.15 'Red-Handed'

**RED:** "I just need something to call you."
**SNOW WHITE:** "Margaret... oh no, Mary, Mary."

**Plot:** After their latest argument, and inspired by August's stories, Ruby quits Granny's Diner and is given a job as Emma's assistant. Meanwhile, a confused David looks for Kathryn, and Ruby finds a box containing a human heart, with Mary Margaret's fingerprints on it.

**Introducing:** We meet Red's love, Peter (Jesse Hutch), who is suspected of being a killer wolf, before the wolf turns out to be someone else entirely.

**Once Upon a Time...** As Red's back-story is explored, her lover, Peter, is suspected of being a wolf who preys on the townspeople. In an unexpected turn of events, the wolf is tragically discovered to be Red herself. Now wanted by the public, she is in danger despite her grandmother's best attempts to protect her. They enlist Snow's help to keep her safe.

**Did You Notice?** August claims he saw Lemurs in Nepal, when in reality they only live in Madagascar – a sign that he is not being completely honest with people.

# 1.16 'Heart of Darkness'

**REGINA**: "Evil doesn't always look evil. Sometimes it's staring right at us, and we don't even realize it."

**Plot:** Emma has to arrest Mary Margaret for the suspected murder of Kathryn Nolan, and Mary Margaret hires Mr. Gold as her defense when the evidence stacks up against her. Henry believes Regina has framed Mary Margaret, and convinces Emma too, but not before Mary Margaret goes missing from her cell.

**Introducing:** In this episode, the focus is on the characters that are already familiar to us, rather than new characters being introduced.

**Once Upon a Time...** Her memory still affected by the potion she took, Snow White sets out to kill the Queen, with Rumplestiltskin's willing help. When Charming tries to stop her – to prevent her from becoming evil herself – he has to take drastic action to make Snow believe him so that their true love can break the spell. When Charming is captured by King George, Snow and her dwarf friends vow to save him.

**Did You Notice?** In his shop Mr. Gold has what appears to be the lamp that contained the Genie (aka the Magic Mirror/Sidney Glass).

# 1.17 'Hat Trick'

**JEFFERSON**: "I know what you refuse to acknowledge, Emma. You're special. You brought something precious to Storybrooke – magic."

**Plot:** Searching for the missing Mary Margaret, Emma is abducted by Jefferson, an apparent madman who is obsessed with hats. When she escapes, she finds the missing Mary Margaret is also imprisoned in his house. Jefferson tries to get Emma to face up to her destiny as the one who will break the Curse. When they eventually overpower Jefferson and get away, Emma persuades Mary Margaret to return to her cell, much to Regina's surprise the next day.

**Introducing:** We are introduced to a Storybrooke resident who, unusually, knows about the Curse and his former life – Jefferson (Sebastian Stan), otherwise known as the Mad Hatter, driven mad by his attempts to recreate his magic hat.

**Once Upon a Time...** For the first time we glimpse yet another world, as we see the Queen enlist the help of the skillful hatter and his magic hat to gain entry into Wonderland, where she outwits the Queen of Hearts to get something she wants. She tricks the Hatter into remaining behind, and after he survives a beheading by the Queen of Hearts, he is left to madly try over and over again to recreate his magic hat to attempt to return to his daughter.

**Did You Notice?** When Jefferson and Grace are at the market, Grace asks if she can buy a stuffed white rabbit doll – a reference to the White Rabbit from *Alice's Adventures in Wonderland*.

# 1.18 'The Stable Boy'

**REGINA**: "Love doesn't work that way. Love, true love, is magic. Not just any magic. The most powerful magic of all. It creates happiness."

**Plot:** Mary Margaret's murder trial continues, as Emma desperately searches for evidence to clear her. August starts to experience problems as his fairy tale self exerts its influence. Regina gloats over Mary Margaret's predicament, but everything changes when Kathryn is discovered alive.

**Introducing:** We finally meet Regina's mother, Cora (Barbara Hershey) in this episode, and the poisoned apple certainly didn't fall far from that tree! We also meet Regina's true love – Daniel (Noah Bean) the handsome stable boy, whose death helped turn Regina into the Evil Queen we know.

**Once Upon a Time...** This episode reveals why Regina hates Snow as much as she does, since it is the young Snow who inadvertently brings about Regina's true love's demise. Despite her later evil actions, it would be difficult not to feel sympathy for Regina here, especially as she is the victim of a scheming maternal figure.

**Did You Notice?** The ring Daniel gives Regina is still with her in Storybrooke. In fact, she later uses it to magically bring the poisoned apple to the real world in 'An Apple Red as Blood.'

## 1.19 'The Return'

REGINA: "You broke our deal."
MR. GOLD: "I broke one deal in my life, dear, and it certainly wasn't this one."

**Plot:** Suspecting he's the Storybrooke counterpart of his son Baelfire, Mr. Gold tries to find out more about August, while August searches for his own father. Regina realizes that Gold has double-crossed her, and makes someone else take the fall for her when Emma investigates her part in framing Mary Margaret. Regina vows to win Henry back.

**Introducing:** Bashful and Happy's Storybrooke counterparts are seen for the first time, at the party to celebrate Mary Margaret's release.

**Once Upon a Time...** In this episode we learn more about Rumplestiltskin's relationship with his son Baelfire after he has become the Dark One. When he breaks a deal he made with his son to rid himself of his magical powers, Rumplestiltskin loses Baelfire and blames the Blue Fairy. Discovering that only the Dark Curse could reunite them, he sows the seeds of sending the inhabitants of Fairy Tale Land to a land without magic.

**Did You Notice?** Mr. Gold finds a wooden donkey in August's room – a reference to the donkeys that bad boys are turned into on Pleasure Island in *Pinocchio*.

## 1.20 'The Stranger'

BLUE FAIRY: "Remember, Pinocchio, be brave, truthful and unselfish. So long as you do that, you will always remain a real boy."

**Plot:** August tries to persuade Emma that she can beat Regina and get custody of Henry in the process. When Mr. Gold refuses to help, Emma finally allows August to tell her his story, and discovers they are more closely linked than she could have imagined, but she still doesn't believe. Meanwhile, Regina tries to seduce David away from Mary Margaret, but fails, and Emma tells Henry they are leaving Storybrooke.

**Introducing:** This episode marks our introduction to Monstro the whale, who swallows Pinocchio and Geppetto in Disney's Pinocchio.

**Once Upon a Time...** We find out how Emma and Pinocchio were saved from the Curse, but Pinocchio broke his promise to his father Geppetto and is now suffering for it, with Emma as his only hope.

**Did You Notice?** The airplane that startles Pinocchio when he arrives in the real world is an Oceanic Airlines flight. Oceanic Airlines is the airline of the pivotal Flight 815 in *Lost*.

## 1.21 'An Apple Red as Blood'

HENRY: "I'm sorry it had to come to this. You may not believe in the Curse or in me, but I believe in you."

**Plot:** Regina notices that the Curse is weakening, and is shocked to find that Mr. Gold wants the Curse to break. He warns her that she'll need to leave town if it happens, as the residents will want revenge. Regina enlists Jefferson's help to use the last of her magic to retrieve a deadly weapon from the other world. When Emma concedes to Regina and agrees to leave Storybrooke, Henry takes a life-threatening risk to prove to her that his stories are true.

**Introducing:** The poisoned apple the Queen had Hansel and Gretel steal from the Blind Witch was earlier seen in 'True North,' but this is the first time we see it in action, as Snow bites into it in Fairy Tale Land to save Charming, and Henry eats an apple turnover made out of it in Storybrooke to convince Emma of the truth.

**Once Upon a Time...** We see Snow leading the forces of good against the Queen to rescue Charming from her clutches. Agreeing to parley with the Queen, Snow bites into the poisoned apple in order to save Charming.

**Did You Notice?** There is a spinning wheel in Mr. Gold's pawnshop, presumably the one Rumplestiltskin used to spin the straw into gold in the fairy tale of the same name.

# 1.22 'A Land Without Magic'

**MOTHER SUPERIOR/BLUE FAIRY:** "If I were you, your Majesty, I'd find a place to hide."

**Plot:** With Henry's life in the balance, Emma and Regina realize they will have to set their differences aside and work together to save him. They go to Mr. Gold for help, and he tells her where a 'true love' potion is hidden that will save Henry. In a game-changing moment for the series, Emma finally believes. Emma slays the dragon Maleficent to get the potion, but Gold double-crosses her and keeps it for himself. When it appears Henry has died, Emma awakens him with true love's kiss, and Storybrooke's inhabitants remember their pasts. After being reunited with Belle, Gold uses the true love potion to bring magic to the town.

**Introducing:** We'd met Regina's frenemy Maleficent before in her human form (in 'The Thing You Love Most'), but in this episode we see her as a dragon. She proves to be a deadly enemy, but Emma triumphs over her in the end thanks to a timely sword throw.

**Once Upon a Time...** Charming escapes the Evil Queen's castle with the Huntsman's help, and vows to find Snow White, with Rumplestiltskin's assistance, on condition that Charming hides the true love potion in the dragon's belly. He does so, and finds Snow, waking her with true love's kiss. They resolve to take back the kingdom and deal with both King George and the Evil Queen.

**Did You Notice?** In the mental hospital, the next cell over from Belle's is labeled S. Glass – indicating Regina had Sidney Glass put there after he disappointed her.

# All That Glitters...

WHETHER HE'S PLAYING THE GLEEFULLY WICKED RUMPLESTILTSKIN, OR HIS MORE URBANE STORYBROOKE COUNTERPART, MR. GOLD, ROBERT CARLYLE ALWAYS SPINS HIS PERFORMANCE INTO PURE MAGIC ON SCREEN IN *ONCE UPON A TIME*. WE CAUGHT UP WITH THE ACCLAIMED ACTOR TO TALK ABOUT RUMPLESTILTSKIN'S PAINFUL PAST, THE MAKE-UP PROCESS USED TO TRANSFORM HIM INTO THE SCALY VILLAIN, AND HOW RUMPLESTILTSKIN IS JUST LIKE A CHILD…

Words: Tara Bennett

**R**obert Carlyle is an actor known for taking risks. Be it on stage or in film, the Scottish actor has earned a stellar reputation for his fearless performances, whether he's playing a violent sociopath in *Trainspotting*, a down on his luck guy who goes *au naturelle* to make ends meet in *The Full Monty*, or even a Bond villain who can't feel pain in *The World Is Not Enough*. Carlyle pushes himself to go wherever his character leads him with refreshing abandon, and that's why he's the perfect man to get inside the tortured skins of Rumplestiltskin/Mr. Gold in *Once Upon a Time*.

While the two versions of the character are connected by their wounded souls, outwardly Carlyle brings them to life as complete opposites. Where Rumple is full of theatrical braggadocio with bite, Mr. Gold is instead a tailored and refined menace whose power is tempered by regret. Yet Carlyle finds a human through-line to connect his performances and in two seasons, while Rumplestiltskin/Mr. Gold may be the villains of the piece, the actor maintains the tricky tightrope of earning the audience's ire and sympathy.

In our exclusive chat with Carlyle, the always affable actor and devoted family man says from the moment he first read the Pilot script he knew *Once*

*Upon a Time* was special. "I was just completely taken by it," he remembers. Fresh off a two season run in Vancouver, B.C. as Dr. Nicholas Rush on the TV series *SGU: Stargate Universe*, Carlyle says he initially thought his North America TV days were over. "I had several independent film offers lined up that would allow me to go home [to Scotland]," he details, but then *Once Upon a Time* changed everything.

"I just got it completely," he enthuses. "I loved the emotion of the fairy tale world and the real world, and the stories being told concurrently. But then the most astonishing thing of all, from my perspective, is that not only was it shooting back in Vancouver where *SGU* was shot, and at the same studios, but it was also on the same stage as *Stargate*! So something was telling me to be here. I'm not the most spiritual man in the world, but there's a little bit of that in me and I couldn't ignore something like that. Even the offices that *Once Upon a Time* use are the old *Stargate* offices. In episode two of Season One ['The Thing You Love Most'], when Rumplestiltskin fell, that set was built on exactly the same set as Rush's quarters," he relates incredulously. "So I guess it's a home away from home."

On another personal note, Carlyle says *Once Upon a Time* also appealed to him because it's a project he can actually share with his three children. Usually a fixture of more adult fare, Carlyle laughs, "Yeah, most of my films can't be seen by my children, so I think it's wonderful. I didn't realize too that the time slot we have used to be the slot for *The Wonderful World of Disney* [TV series], which ran for years.

"I don't think ABC ever really managed to replace that show with a similar family-friendly thing until now, so that's one of the great things about our show, for sure. It works across the board. I remember watching the Pilot episode with my wife, my mother-in-law, and my three kids. They all enjoyed it and loved it for different reasons. It made me realize 'this has got something, this has actually got something.' And of course, I'm a family man myself, so that makes me feel fantastic. So many people come up to me on the street, even here in Vancouver,

## "I THOUGHT I COULDN'T POSSIBLY JUST GIVE ANY KIND OF NATURALISTIC PERFORMANCE. IT JUST WOULDN'T WORK; IT HAD TO BE HEIGHTENED."

and say, 'Thank you so much for making a show my whole family can watch,' so it's lovely."

A long-time fixture in the British theater world, Carlyle has tackled his fair share of iconic, theatrical characters, but in taking on Rumple and Gold, he admits it took him a long time to get the right tone and timbre of each character right in his own mind. "I went around asking my friends and my kids, 'Who is Rumplestiltskin?' It was the only question I had, and everyone smiled and said, 'Oh, yeah! Rumplestiltskin…' and then they didn't know what to say. All they really knew is the really unusual name and that he can spin straw into gold. That

is it. So I thought this is a completely blank canvas. And then, the words I was presented with by Eddy and Adam were so ripe for playing with, so I thought I couldn't possibly just give any kind of naturalistic performance. It just wouldn't work; it had to be heightened.

"So of the three major things that go into Rumplestiltskin," the actor details, "first was the make-up. There is such a massive amount of make-up that when you put it on it is like a mask. I did a lot of workshops with masks many years ago at drama school and that put me in really good stead. There's something quite interesting when you put a mask on your face… you can lose yourself. It makes you almost braver and you can find yourself doing things you might not do if you showed your face."

He continues, "Then I combined the mask work with different types of movement. The one that helped me was looking to the [Italian performance style] Commedia dell'Arte, which tells of farce. The way those characters stand and pose really goes hand in hand with the costuming the show had in mind, so it all fit very well. And the Commedia dell'Arte is all about using masks as well, so it all started to make sense when I landed on that.

"Then the thing that completed it all was that you can't have these extraordinary masks and these wonderful flourishes of movement and speak like this [referring to his natural Glaswegian accent]," he laughs. "I had to change my voice somehow. I tried many, many different tones, but the one thing that I found that did it for me was hearing my son. If anyone becomes an actor, it's going to be him because he's always acting and changing his voice. He does this little thing [Robert raises his pitch and babbles like Rumplestiltskin]... so Rumplestiltskin is like a child. He loves the mischief and dragging people along so far and then stabbing a knife in their back. He's very child-like in the way he does his deals, so those were the three things that really gave me the part."

With a pause, he then adds, "I have a great love of British comic actors of the late 1960s, so there are little bits of those guys in him too. I knew the character

"WITH RUMPLESTILTSKIN, IT'S USUALLY ABOUT GETTING SOMEONE A DEAL AND THERE'S NOT MUCH HE CAN DO ABOUT THE REPERCUSSIONS."

## Did You Know?

• Robert was awarded the OBE (Officer of the Order of the British Empire) by Queen Elizabeth II in 1999 for services to Drama.

• In 1991, Robert founded the theater company Raindog (named after a favorite album by the singer Tom Waits) in Glasgow with some actor friends. As well as producing successful theatrical productions, the company also branched into television and film production, including the award-winning 2009 movie *Wasted*.

needed to be fun or you wouldn't accept him. For me, he's the fun in the show. We all love the bad guy. He's done tongue-in-cheek and I think it's okay. Little kids are a wee bit scared by Rumple, but are still excited when they see him," he chuckles.

Circling back to his make-up, Carlyle admits that aspect of Rumple is often the most fascinating to those that come up to him asking about the extent of it all (it's even inside his mouth) and how he deals with the process. "Obviously, I'm in the hands of some very good make-up artists," he says. "It's been a collaboration, and my contribution to the make-up since episode one, Season One has just been to add a little more of this, a little less of that, a few additions here, and more darkness there, so I can see the character coming alive as it's being applied. It's very much like putting a mask on, and when you do mask work, you're supposed to stare in the mirror at your face for a long while, then put the mask on and look back and you can see someone else there. Now it's at a point when I can see if we need more black in the teeth or the eyeliner. It's the little touches that go a long way."

And Rumple remains quite the process, even two years into the character. "Originally, it took about two and a half hours," Carlyle says of the make-up application time, "but now we have it down to about an hour. Mr. Gold is easy. Fantastic! No problems there. With Rumple, there's an awful lot that I have to be helped into, so that whole process takes a half hour. And what people don't understand is that the taking off takes just as long. It's an hour at night to get the whole thing off."

In crafting the many dark, mercurial moods of his characters, Carlyle explains, "The first thing that gets you when you are playing a villain is that villains don't know they're wrong. They don't think they're a villain. Most of the [scenes] I've played, especially with Mr. Gold, is projecting that, 'You knew this was coming.' He's always got an answer. With Rumplestiltskin, it's usually about getting someone a deal and there's not much he can do about the repercussions. The amazing thing about Eddy and Adam's writing is that no matter how vile and horrible some of the things he might do are, he can look back and say with a clear mind, 'You should have looked at the details there, and maybe not gone this way.'"

But Carlyle says the real saving grace for his character has been the revelations about his past, which have steered him away from just being a bad guy. "For me, I loved 'Desperate Souls' where you find out about his boy and his humble beginnings, and then 'Skin Deep,' which changed everything. From there, I could feel from the outside a real change towards Rumplestiltskin. People at that point suddenly saw he has a heart. Belle (Emilie de Ravin) began to peel away some of his mask. With the kiss, she peels away the mask and you see the person, a nice guy with his boy. I think from that point on people looked at Rumplestiltskin with a different eye."

However, that doesn't mean audiences aren't thoroughly frustrated with Rumple/Gold for often making really poor decisions that deter him from a true road to redemption. "I think it's wonderful," Carlyle laughs with glee at his character's shortcomings. "The way that the character is written he doesn't do exactly what you want him to do. Especially for people who are obsessed with his relationship with Belle and their love story, he just doesn't do things right. He's kind of incapable. If you think, this man has been alive for three hundred

"RUMPLESTILTSKIN IS LIKE A CHILD. HE LOVES THE MISCHIEF AND DRAGGING PEOPLE ALONG SO FAR AND THEN STABBING A KNIFE IN THEIR BACK. HE'S VERY CHILD-LIKE IN THE WAY HE DOES HIS DEALS."

years, and he's had one love in his life – his wife – so he doesn't know how to do it [well]. When things go wrong, you should almost expect it. But on the outside, I feel people really are desperate for their love story [to go well], but I don't think Adam, Eddy, and certainly myself, are ever going to make that easy. We're all going to have to wait for that."

The actor also warns that Rumple/Gold's path back to his son Baelfire (played by Dylan Schmid as a young boy, and Michael Raymond-James as an adult) will also be a journey fraught with many complications. "I think the quest to find his son has always, always been what it's

all been about for him," Carlyle muses. "The moment he let his son's hand go in the vortex in episode 19 ['The Return'], from that point he's been trying to find him and get him back. In 'The Crocodile' he tells it all to Belle and what his whole life has been about. In my own opinion looking at it, no matter who comes in front of him, none of those characters matter to Rumplestiltskin. What matters is finding his boy. Losing him ruined his entire life."

Carlyle smiles and admits, "I think there will be hours of television to get him anywhere near reconciliation with his son... *if* he ever gets that." ✤

# Setting the Scene

FROM MEDIEVAL HOVELS TO TOWERING CASTLES AND ECLECTIC APARTMENTS, THE SETS OF *ONCE UPON A TIME* ARE CREATED THANKS TO THE TALENTS OF PRODUCTION DESIGNER MICHAEL JOY AND SET DECORATOR MARK LANE. HERE THEY TELL US ABOUT THEIR WORK IN BUILDING UP THE WORLD OF THE SHOW...

Words: Bryan Cairns

Green screen in action – a work-in-progress of the beanstalk sequence from "Tallahassee"

**S**cour the Earth all you want, but there is absolutely no place like *Once Upon a Time*'s Fairy Tale Land or Storybrooke anywhere. That's why the show's magnificent castles, comfy quarters and dingy dungeons have been erected at Vancouver's Bridge Studios. It's within these soundstages that Production Designer Michael Joy and Set Decorator Mark Lane have carefully crafted the bulk of the environments required for the realm-trotting TV series.

"A production designer is the person who is in charge of the overall look of the picture," explains Joy. "That includes all the sets, locations, the props, anything that's going to be added afterwards in post[-production] and providing visual material, so that everybody knows what the physical stuff is actually going to look like. I give direction to the set dresser, so he can go out and buy the stuff to decorate.

"Mostly what I do is identify all the things that are new," continues Joy about his approach. "In a lot of the scripts, we're just re-juggling stuff that we've already seen before. I separate all the stuff that's new and try to figure out some way to take it to a place even cooler than deemed possible. I use the writing as a jumping-off point."

It helps that Joy and Lane have a history. Eight years ago, the two of them worked together on a David Hasselhoff-starring TV movie, *Avalanche*, and quite simply clicked. Since then, they've collaborated on numerous projects and developed a professional shorthand.

"The other day, we were walking away from one of the sets," recalls Lane. "We weren't finishing each other's sentences, but we realized when it comes to the sets and what needs to be done, our department is able to fulfill it pretty easily without Michael having to go into a lot of detail. He trusts what we do, and we have a pretty good idea of what he wants most of the time."

That synergy is a welcome bonus and makes the workday smoother. However, the series still has its own challenges that factor into the equation.

"We shoot so much on the stage, so one of the challenges is to keep all those

> "WE GO BACK AND
> FORTH IN TIME, SO WE
> CHERRY PICK LOOKS
> THAT WILL BE THE
> MOST SURPRISING AND
> VISUALLY DELIGHTFUL."
> — MICHAEL JOY

Fairy Tale Land past - the Blind Witch's Gingerbread Cottage

The Evil Queen's Hall of Mirrors

stylistic balls in the air," says Joy. "We have Fairy Tale Land present. We have Fairy Tale Land past. In each episode, we sometimes go to different parts of Fairy Tale Land. We also try to give it many different looks. We've done a Fairy Tale Land which is deep in the dark forest, and one that is almost in Southern Italy. We've done Fairy Tale Land in a Chinese village. It's just mixing it up. We've done a seaside town. We go back and forth in time, so we cherry pick looks that will be the most surprising and visually delightful."

Lane adds, "The biggest challenge is anything to do with medieval or any land we go to, there's not a lot of dressing or furniture [available] for it. We have to make a lot of stuff. We spend a lot of time on the internet scouring for stuff that other people have made that we can bring in. There are a few prop houses in town that have collections from over the years of other shows that have had different time periods. As far as the sets themselves, the biggest challenge is when we do the green screen. Basically, we put elements in the middle of it and then have to look at the Zeus [software] system on a monitor to see where our stuff fits, to make sure it's not intersecting with walls and other stuff. With the green screen, you're not within built walls or in a castle somewhere."

*Once Upon a Time*'s hectic schedule doesn't always allow new sets to be constructed from scratch. In order to beat the clock and maximize the budget, the production team often re-imagines existing pieces to better suit their needs.

> ## "BECAUSE REGINA BROUGHT THE CURSE, SHE WAS IMMUNE TO IT. IN THE SAME WAY SHE DRESSED FOR SUCCESS, WE MADE THE DECISION THAT SHE DECORATED BOTH HER HOUSE AND OFFICE FOR SUCCESS."
>
> ### – MICHAEL JOY

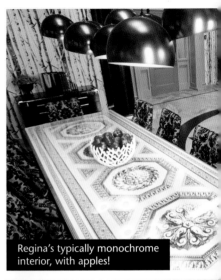

Regina's typically monochrome interior, with apples!

"We have a standing set for a tavern we built for episode 105 ["That Still Small Voice"] and we've probably shot in it 12 times for different locations," reveals Joy. "We just move the walls around or add a fireplace. Another set we constantly shoot in is a cave set. We put rails and mining carts in it. We've made it a prison and six different dungeons. We just have to be clever about repurposing the stuff we have."

"We do a lot of hovels, which are like medieval cottages," adds Lane. "We'll use items again and again. We try to change it up as much as possible. In broader strokes, we'll do something different like curtains and rugs."

Regina's castle, as well as that of Charming and Snow, are two of 14 permanent structures. Both are like night and day, contrasting with one another and encapsulating the series' Good vs. Evil theme.

"I decided to make the Evil Queen's castle industrial with concrete and metal, and really make it of a dark design," says Joy. "We designed it and episodes later, we found out that she hadn't really designed it. She had married a guy [King Leopold] and it was already his castle, so we had to do a happier one. Her castle is sort of a 19th Century version made out of iron and steel. Then on the outside, we tried to make it this spikey, lotus-flower design, so it looked contemporary, like a modern building."

"When we were doing the Queen's castle, the dressing was darker in color and less soft in shape," adds Lane.

"Michael's architecture was quite pointed and jagged, whereas with Snow and Charming's, there was a lot more bedding, and color, and soft furnishings, and warmer tones."

Regina's grand Storybrooke abode is no less spectacular, with its abundant space, detailed interiors, marbled floors and layered textures. It clearly makes a statement, which is exactly the point. Joy and Lane further incorporated elements that would reflect Regina's distinct personality.

"The idea going into Storybrooke was it was under this Curse, but because Regina brought the Curse, she was immune to it," explains Joy. "In the same way she dressed for success, we made the decision that she decorated both her house and office for success. It's very imperial in the tradition of [designer] David Hicks and the great decorators of the 20th Century. We made a conscious decision to keep her palette super defined with a black and white look. It dramatizes her need for control with a limited palette and very rigid color scheme. It's just a very classic approach to interior design."

"Regina's office was the one we took the most amount of time with and really pored over," elaborates Lane. "The only punch of color in the whole room is her apples. That was a different sort of challenge because there are so many shades of black and white, so you were constantly trying to make sure everything was in harmony."

In comparison to Regina's residence, all the other houses and homes seem

The Evil Queen's lair

The Evil Queen's dark, industrial-looking castle

Mary Margaret's crafty, rustic apartment

downright understated. In Mary Margaret's case, her roomy apartment has a rustic charm to it. The decor is whimsical, but also extremely white.

"The idea is Mary Margaret is very earthy," reports Joy. "Her place is supposed to be a loft. The bones of it were an industrial space or an old office space. She's very crafty, and because she's a teacher who does crafts with her kids, she took the same do-it-yourself approach to decorating her home. You could imagine she decorated that all by going to thrift sales. It's meant to be an echo of who she was as a romantic character living in the woods. The fact that it's kind of a modern-day princess type of environment also echoes the character we didn't know existed in the beginning."

Mr. Gold's pawn shop is another recognizable visual anchor. Overflowing with strange objects, everything in that establishment has been bartered for or from somebody who owes him. Negotiating with Gold is like making a deal with the devil and in many ways, the gloomy place successfully feels... sinister.

"It was never supposed to be a standing set, which it is now," says Lane. "Again, because it was in one of the first episodes, everything we brought in there we rented. We filled it and then they decided it was going to keep coming back, so we needed to start purchasing all this stuff. Basically, over the first season, and even into the second one, we've been replacing it bit-by-bit. For us, it wasn't about going out

and getting a bunch of antiques and throwing them in. Everything has a purpose in there. Nothing went in that wasn't completely thought out."

Plenty of *Once Upon a Time*'s sets are virtual or digitally enhanced. It can sometimes get a little technological, which is perhaps why Joy cites Red and Granny's practical locations as some of his favorites.

"Originally, there was just Granny's Bed & Breakfast," he explains. "I imagined we would need a set where people from the town would come to and gather and interact. We didn't really have a place in Storybrooke they could gather. So it's meant to be a cozy coffee shop where people go to have coffee, pie, and gossip. The form of it was to be a classic diner from the 30s or 40s, that had slowly been upgraded. If you look closer, there's the tree motif wallpaper which we deliberately put on all the walls of the original set, to tie Storybrooke to the forest.

"Then we have Red's cabin," he continues. "The exterior of that was stylistically based on Norwegian churches. By the time we finished designing it, it sort of had a bit of a Japanese vibe to it. I don't know quite how that happened, but it was a mash-up of Japanese and Norwegian. It really felt like a beautiful, northern mythical cabin. Then when you went inside, it was all this pickled wood. It really was like it was in another place and time."

Moving from one place in time to another when this interview was conducted, Lane was prepping to return to Dr. Whale's old stomping grounds.

"We built the inside of Frankenstein's lab," notes Lane. "We're doing a big virtual set, which is the interior of Frankenstein's father's house, in a big drawing room with a giant Christmas tree.

"As far as the castle [goes], we took Frankenstein's lab and made it twice as big," he continues. "There was a slightly steampunk element to the whole thing. It didn't feel like it had a German or Austrian vibe to it; it had a slight edge to it."

As for the mandatory mad scientist paraphernalia, "You would be surprised

Dr. Frankenstein's electrifying castle!

Granny's Diner

Red's cabin

The entrance to the Queen of Hearts' maze in Wonderland

what you can find online," Lane shares. "There was some stuff in town. But we manufactured a lot of his lab, like the bubbling stuff and cylinders."

"We also did a version of Wonderland on *Once Upon a Time*, which was a fun episode. A lot of that set was CG. All the stuff in Jefferson's house was all a set on stage. Jefferson's living room was location. Once he jumped into the hat and went through the mirror, all of that was set extensions. All of the hedges we built. The platform that the Queen of Hearts was sitting on was real. It's always a bit of a mix. It's never just the actors standing on a green box."

Joy and Lane work tirelessly at their jobs. The other night, Lane was filming until 5am. Despite the long hours, *Once Upon a Time* is a treasure trove of creativity and energy. At the end of the day, there's nowhere else Lane would rather be.

"Standing in the middle of a set, whether it's a medieval tavern or a hovel or a gingerbread house, it's about forgetting there's a studio outside of the walls," he concludes. "It's just this feeling you're in the middle of a Disney ride and that makes you feel like a kid again."

85

So Ch

AS SNOW WHITE'S TRUE LOVE, PRINCE CHARMING HAS PROVEN THAT HE WILL ALWAYS FIND HER, NO MATTER WHAT THE OBSTACLE – A CONVICTION THAT HAS OFTEN BEEN TESTED. ACTOR JOSH DALLAS TELLS US ABOUT PLAYING THE HERO FOR WHOM THE COURSE OF TRUE LOVE DOESN'T ALWAYS RUN SMOOTHLY...

Words: Tara Bennett

# arming!

In most fairy tale stories, Prince Charming is the dashing hero that rushes in during the last act of the story to save his princess so they can live happily ever after together. In *Once Upon a Time*, Prince Charming is certainly heroic, but he has this chronic problem of getting his heart's desire, only to have it yanked away a short time after. Whether it's slipping into a coma and losing his memory completely thanks to the Evil Queen's dark curse, or watching his reunited adult daughter and wife spirited away from him to Fairy Tale Land, Charming isn't always the luckiest of men.

Actor Josh Dallas who plays Prince Charming/

David Nolan chuckles at that description of his character, "Yeah, I'm going to have to talk to [executive producers] Eddy and Adam about this," he concedes with a hearty laugh. "They give Charming something and then they take it away. But it shows Charming's resolve [facing] the things that happen in his life and how he deals with them. He's trying to do the best he can."

A good man trying to overcome some trying circumstances is a pretty accurate read on what *Once Upon a Time*'s Prince Charming had been dealing with before and during the 28 years of the Storybrooke curse. As David Nolan, he made a lot of poor choices and mistakes with his life, which made the character

"BECAUSE OF THE CURSE HE WAS A MAN WHO COULDN'T COMMIT AND FOLLOW THROUGH ON HIS WORD, WHICH IS THE DIRECT OPPOSITE TO WHAT CHARMING WOULD HAVE DONE IN FAIRY TALE LAND."

much more nuanced than the perfect, idealized prince of the classic tale.

Dallas, who was a member of the famed Royal Shakespeare Company in England, says *Once Upon a Time* is a dream vehicle for actors because it takes traditional storytelling to a whole new place.

"We're telling people the sides to these characters that they didn't know," Dallas says of the show's alt take on classic stories. "For me, it was the chance to make Prince Charming, somehow, jump off the page a little more and make him more relevant, and more human. We can show [the characters] in a new light and play them differently, and more up-to-date. As far as Eddy and Adam go, it takes people of great taste to sift through all of those years of different artists' interpretations of these characters and be able to change it, make it up to date, make it cool, make it our own and make it cinematic. I think they do that brilliantly."

*Once Upon a Time* is Dallas' first regular television series after guest spots on series like *Hawaii Five-0*, *CSI: Crime Scene Investigation*, and *Doctor Who*, and movies such as *Thor* and *Red Tails*, and he knew he made the right career choice when he won the role of the flawed hero. "With our Prince Charming, throughout the entire first season I got to play a side to him that was completely un-charming," he laughs. "Because of the curse he was a man who couldn't commit and follow through on his word, which is the direct opposite to what Charming would have done in Fairy Tale Land. I wanted to show him with all of his flaws, to the hilt. I wanted to show the extremes between the two personalities. You just had to go for it when he was giving Mary Margaret the wrong card, or when he couldn't support her, because that was his curse. It was his curse to be dishonest and not forthright to keep him away from his one true love."

Dallas says getting to play a season full of bad choices in Storybrooke made his Fairy Tale Land persona even more interesting. "As actors, we have all this back-story of the last 28 years, plus the fairy tale characters, so that informs them as full characters. Like David says in episode two of season two ['We Are Both'], when he's giving the speech to Storybrooke: 'We are both now and that makes us richer and better for it.' Now in season two, it's a great chance for David in Storybrooke to have all of who he used to be in Fairy Tale Land enter into him, which makes him [well-rounded] and more aware of who he is. He made mistakes because he's human and it's great for us as actors to be able to play that. And what's also great about the show is that it's completely un-cynical about love. I don't think there are many television shows that take that view of love. We show it for all of its glory and all of its greatness. I love that, and as we say, true love is magic as well. There's nothing more powerful in the world."

With the curse broken at the start of season two, all of the actors have had to merge their dual identities, a turn of events that Dallas says he "finds very freeing" because Charming "has

knowledge of both lives now, which makes the knowledge richer of who he is as a man. I think it's wonderful because now he has kind of a redemption path for David Nolan in Storybrooke. He can try, with his actions, to rewrite some of the wrongs David Nolan created in season one. He can try to get back on track as much as possible."

As everyone knows, Charming had to do most of that alone with Snow and Emma stuck in Fairy Tale Land for half the season. So instead of moping, Charming took action and filled Emma's role as Sheriff, helping calm and guide his town as they dealt with the myriad of post-curse repercussions. Dallas says it was just another exercise in patience for the man and the couple. "He's there until Emma gets back because he's so sure and confident that he will always find Snow. He will always find her because that's the way true love works, even if it's a struggle. The Storybrooke people are confused about why they can't cross the line, and what does magic mean there now. So he had to take control and he told them, 'If you want me to lead you, I will be here and get my family back and help you get back yours.' He was on a mission."

Often times a Charming mission involves some kind of action, with a fight, or a chase, or even slaying a dragon. Dallas says filming the latter moment was one of his favorites, if only because of the absurdity behind the eventual coolness of it onscreen once the VFX of the dragon was added over the rather more prosaic-looking prop. "[The prop I filmed on] looked like a gigantic Kosher dill pickle that I was jumping onto," he laughs. "It was like I was at one of those bronco bars with a huge, green pickle. It just reminded me it's the best job in the world because you get to play and use your imagination all day long, acting like you're killing dragons. I'm a 30-year-old man acting like he's 12."

In the same episode, he also loved facing off with steel against Rumplestiltskin in Fairy Tale Land. "To work all day with Bobby Carlyle is the best," Dallas enthuses. "I loved that sword fight. I love doing all of

"WE'RE TELLING PEOPLE THE SIDES TO THESE CHARACTERS THAT THEY DIDN'T KNOW. FOR ME, IT WAS THE CHANCE TO MAKE PRINCE CHARMING, SOMEHOW, JUMP OFF THE PAGE A LITTLE MORE AND MAKE HIM MORE RELEVANT, AND MORE HUMAN."

that stuff. The more they give me, the happier I am."

He adds that another favorite action moment goes back to the pilot "It was the scene with the baby in my arms. It was Prince Charming at his most heroic in defending his child, wanting to save her life and his wife's future. It was a strong moment for Charming... and then he was put in a coma," he laughs.

Asked about some of the moments that propelled Charming forward this season, Dallas says being a surrogate parent for Henry has been a highlight. "It's been his chance to be the father that he wasn't for 28 years. Even though he put Emma in that wardrobe to save her life and save the entire kingdom, he missed her growing up and being a father. In that true Charming way, he's going to try to do the best that he can through Henry for Emma. He doesn't always get it right. He doesn't always go about it the right

# Did You Know?

• In the Disney animated *Snow White and the Seven Dwarfs*, Prince Charming was voiced by actor and singer Harry Stockwell, who performed the song "One Song," about Charming's true love for Snow White.

• In the original fairy tale by the Brothers Grimm, Prince Charming was not named as such. Charming is a name that developed from subsequent adaptations and retellings of the story.

"WHAT'S ALSO GREAT ABOUT THE SHOW IS THAT IT'S COMPLETELY UN-CYNICAL ABOUT LOVE. I DON'T THINK THERE ARE MANY TELEVISION SHOWS THAT TAKE THAT VIEW OF LOVE. WE SHOW IT FOR ALL OF ITS GLORY AND ALL OF ITS GREATNESS."

way, but he's trying. He deeply missed out on being a father – he was one for like, five minutes!" he laughs.

Dallas says during their separation arc, he really loved the moment when he connected to Snow and Emma through the netherworld. "It was a great moment. He has so much faith in Snow that she will be able to figure it out and get back to him.

"Another great episode was "Child of the Moon" with Meghan Ory, who plays Red," he continues. "Snow and Red have a beautiful friendship between two women. But Red kind of becomes Charming's Deputy in Storybrooke, and it becomes a real friendship between a man and a woman, which I don't think you see a lot on television shows. Usually there's something romantic, but they just have a pure friendship like a brother and sister, and

I really like that relationship and I hope that vibe grows more."

After the midseason break, *Once Upon a Time* shifted dramatically again with the return of Snow and Emma to Storybrooke. Charming finally got to be with his wife again, and begin the process of getting to know his long-lost daughter in a brand new way. "Obviously Mary Margaret and Emma have had time to bond while they tried to get out of Fairy Tale Land, but now that they're back, Charming just wants to find out who Emma is as his friend first," the actor explains. "He's trying not to be such a parent figure to her. It's going to come out naturally because she's his daughter, but he wants to get to know her as a woman first and who she is. He wants there to be space and air around that relationship so it can grow into something more important. I think he deeply, deeply respects her as a woman and who she is and who she has become. She's so strong, honorable, smart and beautiful so he's proud of her. I think he's looking forward to

moments when they can truly become friends. I'm hoping there will be some father/daughter police work that needs to be done in Storybrooke so they can work together as a team."

He was also happy to get into Charming's back-story that related to his fallen twin brother, James. "I wanted to go back and fully realize more of Charming's back-story, and his brother is a huge part of that. I wanted to know how is James different having been raised by King George?"

Dallas is clearly a man smitten with his character and job. He laughs as he offers, "Network television with 22 episodes in a season separates the men from the boys for sure! It takes enormous stamina, but what's great about it is that as an actor, and particularly on this show, the characters grow and evolve constantly. They are always pushing the envelope with these characters throughout the season. For an actor, it's a no-brainer to want to be a part of something like this."

# PRODUCING
## The
## Magic

Words: Paul Terry

BEING A PRODUCER FOR A NETWORK TV SERIES IS A DEMANDING JOB. HERE, EXECUTIVE PRODUCER STEVE PEARLMAN AND PRODUCER KATHY GILROY EXPLAIN THE DETAILS BEHIND THEIR MULTIFACETED ROLES, AND HOW THERE IS NEVER A "TYPICAL DAY" ON A SHOW AS BIG AND AS CHALLENGING AS *ONCE UPON A TIME...*

**H**ow did you both end up being transported into the magical *Once* world?
**Steve Pearlman:** I remember it was Super Bowl Sunday in 2011. An agent friend of mine emailed me and said, "What are you doing?" I said, "I'm cleaning up around the house," and he replied, "Well, I'm sending you a script and you have to read it *today*." The agent happened to also be [*Once* co-creators/Executive Producers] Eddy [Kitsis] and Adam [Horowitz]'s agent... and it was the pilot script for *Once Upon a Time*. I read it right away, and emailed him back, saying, "You need to get me on this show." It was one of the most interesting, most exciting and freshest ideas that I'd come across in a long time.

**Kathy Gilroy:** I had been working on another ABC show called *V* with Steve [Pearlman] actually. When he was offered the pilot for *Once Upon a Time*, he put me forward to be the Line Producer for the Pilot episode. Since then we've moved forward into the first and now the second season.

**Steve Pearlman:** Yeah, me and Kathy worked together on *V*, and coincidentally, we'd both worked on another show a number of years back called *Reunion* for the Fox network.

**You've both worked on a huge array of very different TV and film projects. Are there any specific previous experiences from those other gigs that have been useful for working on *Once Upon a Time*?**
**Kathy Gilroy:** As I grew up in Alberta, Canada – and because I've done a few Westerns where I've been an assistant director – that's been very useful with regards to all of the horse work that we do on *Once Upon a Time*. I'm sort of the resident horse person that knows what we can and can't achieve for those scenes. So having that skill has been a great help. It's been one of those funny, specific skills that you learn as a kid growing up in

"THERE REALLY IS NO TYPICAL DAY, WHICH IS PART OF WHAT I LOVE ABOUT THIS JOB."– STEVE PEARLMAN

# PRODUCING ESSENTIALS

**Got aspirations to be a TV producer?** *Once Upon a Time* **Executive Producer STEVE PEARLMAN has some key advice...**

**• Learn about Character, Drama and Structure**

"I'm not a writer, and I've never wanted to be a writer, but I've got background working in TV development, so I have an understanding of story and character. I can read a script and know what is important, and know whether a scene is working or not. Whether you're a writer or not, you need to understand drama and structure. That's something you can learn in film school, but you can also get that by watching a lot of TV and movies. I would always tell interns, 'Watch TV. You can see online every week which are the highest and lowest-rated shows.' I would watch both and figure out for myself, what is it about this show that people are responding to? Or, why would this be the lowest rated show out of 150 on air? Sometimes it's scheduling, sometimes the show is really bad – badly cast, badly written – and a lot of times you can see that." **(Continued overleaf)**

Alberta. It's the first time for a show that we've shot in Vancouver that we've done so much horse work, so that's felt really great and it keeps things exciting for me too, personally.

**Steve Pearlman:** We shot *V* in Vancouver too, and there was a lot of special effects and visual effects on that show, which really laid a lot of the groundwork for the stuff we're doing on *Once Upon a Time*. On *V* we were creating a world largely on a spaceship, and with *Once Upon a Time* we're creating a fairy tale world, but in both cases it's something that's not of *our* world. We worked very closely with the VFX team on *V* and developed a great relationship with them. What that show taught me was a short-hand and an understanding of what you can do with VFX and what the limitations are. It's an ever-evolving process, because technology is changing all the time, and we're always looking to see what we can do to make it better. But working on *V* really opened up a lot of doors for us on this show. Castles don't really exist here. If we had the opportunity to go to Scotland or Ireland or someplace in Eastern Europe and

shoot the show completely on location in real castles, that would be fantastic, but that really wasn't an option for a lot of reasons. Even if we shot the show in LA, there is no sound-stage big enough to shoot the interiors that we've got on this show, so that's what led us to the world of virtual sets. But it's about being able to know where you can make them work, and also where you don't want to use them.

**What is a typical episode experience like for you both in your different producing roles?**
**Kathy Gilroy:** The most intensive part of my job as Line Producer is prepping the upcoming episode. Once we have it out the door and over to the director and the 1st AD [Assistant Director], it's really in their hands then. So from the very first day on a new episode, we'll do a pre-concept meeting. Then, seven days out, we'll do a concept meeting. We'll spend those next seven days trying to figure out how we're going to achieve everything in the script. We look at what we can and can't afford, and sometimes have to

> *"ONCE UPON A TIME WAS ONE OF THE MOST INTERESTING, MOST EXCITING AND FRESHEST IDEAS THAT I'D COME ACROSS IN A LONG TIME."* –
> **STEVE PEARLMAN**

offer alternatives, and we do that whole process every eight days. This means that every eight-day cycle we get a new director, and we spend the next eight days trying to figure out how we're actually going to achieve bringing the script that the guys have written into a reality. So every single day is full of prep, scouting for locations and also castings. Once the process gets into the post-production stage, it's really a matter of managing the visual effects. We have to look at how much has changed/increased from what we initially planned. It's crucial to figure out how much everything is costing from that point on, and carefully managing that.

**Steve Pearlman:** There really is no typical day, which is part of what I love about this job. Yesterday I got up at 5am and had to be at work at 6am, and we were on set. Today, we were on location, and on Friday we have a late call so I probably won't even go into work until 11am. Some days I'm on location all day, and other days I'm in the office or the studio. So I'm bouncing all over the place, all the time. I'm also moving back and forth between the episodes. At any given time we're prepping an episode, shooting another, editing an episode, plus, we've got VFX that are being emailed to us for approval, constantly. Then we're dealing with new episodes before

### • Organization and Decision-Making

"In terms of personal qualities, be organized. There's a lot going on. You have to be able to make decisions. And you have to be able to stand by those decisions. I've got 150 people on crew, plus the cast, who I'm interfacing with on a daily basis. If you make a decision – or you don't make one or are wishy-washy about it – they're gonna lose respect for you."

### • Multi-tasking and Focus

"You really have to be able to juggle a lot of different things. When you're on set you have to be pretty focused on that episode. If one of the actors, or the director, has any questions, which could simply be, 'Why am I picking this thing up?' you need to know why, especially if we have a director who has not worked on the show before. They might not understand all of the mythology, or some of the camera conventions that we do or do not do on *Once*. You have to be pretty focused on what's immediately in front of you. If you're in a prep meeting for the next episode, and someone asks a question that needs feedback, it will be because they need to find or buy something – they will need answers. It's my job to have the answers, or figure out what the answer is. Saying, 'I don't know,' is not usually a good answer." **(Continued overleaf)**

they go into the prep stage. I would say, at any given time, I'm very deeply involved with about five to six episodes. You've got to keep that all straight in your head. On average, which is typical of TV production, you're looking at a 12-hour day minimum – some days are 16 or 17 hours long.

**Kathy Gilroy:** Episodic television is a bit of a treadmill, but if you create a system and a routine that you stick with, it makes it easier for all the department heads, and ultimately, makes it easier for you. Simple things like having the meetings on the same days in the prep schedule helps a lot. The production meeting is always two days out from shooting. Sticking with that routine as best you can is part of the success of a show. There are so many details involved, that if we didn't have some kind of regular routine, we'd implode.

**Going back to the first season, what are you most proud of, looking back?**

**Steve Pearlman:** The first season was a real challenge because *everything* was new. In every episode there was at least one element that became a very big challenge that we would have to figure out. We were doing things that really aren't typically done in episodic television, like Pinocchio and Geppetto on a raft in the middle of the ocean being chased by a whale!

**Kathy Gilroy:** That Pinocchio episode ['The Stranger'], with all of the water, we're enormously proud of that.

**Steve Pearlman:** Or something like a burning building in Storybrooke – that was a huge challenge. The building we needed to burn was a national historic site in British Columbia, so we couldn't put real fire in there. We also did an episode that involved three kids under the age of 12, and that became a logistical challenge because there are limited hours that they can work.

**Kathy Gilroy:** A lot of the sequences with the Evil Queen's carriage, those as well. To be able to get the chance to do these sorts of things in TV is so rare, and it looks great.

# "WE'RE CONSTANTLY BRINGING NEW FAIRY TALE CHARACTERS INTO THE MIX, AND THAT'S INTERESTING TO ME." – KATHY GILROY

**Steve Pearlman:** And of course, we did the Season One finale with a dragon! There was a specific shot where Josh Dallas (Prince Charming) had to jump onto the back of the CG dragon. So challenges on this show may end up being something that was invisible to the audience, or a big sequence that has one shot in it that we spent more time talking about than any other VFX sequence.

**And how about Season Two so far?**
**Steve Pearlman:** Season Two has been a little bit easier as we had 22 episodes under our belt from last year. That means we can revisit some of the things that we've done in the past and say, "We know how to do that now." There have been some things that have been bigger challenges for us though, like Captain Hook's boat.
**Kathy Gilroy:** Yes! We had a lot of challenges getting the ship into the country, because it's an American-based ship. We had a couple of sleepless nights trying to figure it out and negotiate with Transport Canada to make sure that they were satisfied and we were following their rules and regulations. They were enormously helpful, because obviously we don't bring a ship across the border every single day! So far for me that has been the most logistically challenging, but it looked amazing. It was worth every moment of pain. Especially because it was all real. We were doing camera boat-to-ship shots, and all of that stuff that looks fantastic.
**Steve Pearlman:** Yeah, it was a little bit hairy there for 24 hours! But then the problem beyond that was we were bringing Hook into Storybrooke, and he was going to be a bigger part of our show… but we didn't have access to that ship anymore. The one we'd used had a previous obligation to be in the San Francisco area during the winter for a variety of engagements. That left us with a character who we wanted to play a

### • Problem-Solving

"A lot of what I do on a daily basis, if you take the specifics of it, is problem-solving. It's figuring out how to make a script that everybody loves work for the budget or the schedule that we have. Or if we've got actors who need to be in New York for publicity, or in LA for something, or family obligations, you solve that. We try and honor that – the cast is here in Vancouver, away from their homes and families – so if they have a family event that they need to get to, we try our best to accommodate that. You have to figure all of that out so that the studio and the network still get a show of the quality they're expecting."

### • Self-motivation and Determination

"You've got to push yourself, because there are too many people out there that want to get into this business. Today, you can go out to a store and buy a HD camera, shoot, and edit on your laptop. If you want to show people that you're a good director, you can show them. Back in the day, you had to go and find an editing console, rent a camera, etc. The opportunities for access to equipment, or even developing the writing side – a lot is happening through the internet – is so much greater than even 10 years ago. If you're sitting back waiting for somebody to find you, they're not going to find you."

bigger role in the show, but we didn't have his ship. So we actually built a pirate ship in three weeks. It's quite expensive, and it's a set, so it's not a real ship. We built it on a barge so we can float it out into the water and we've been shooting scenes on it. It's docked in the harbor out in the town where we film Storybrooke.

**Which character dynamics are your loved ones enjoying the most at this point in *Once Upon a Time*'s story?**

**Kathy Gilroy:** So many! My dad loves Rumplestiltskin. But overall, it's amazing the amount of people that have come to me to say how much they've related to an individual character.

**Steve Pearlman:** I have two teenage sons, and their favorite character is Rumplestiltskin, just because he's fun, unpredictable, dangerous, and dark. Robert Carlyle is

fantastic and everything he does with that character is so much fun to watch.

**Kathy Gilroy:** For me it's been more about the group as a whole, and I've just been amazed at how many characters we've brought in. We're constantly bringing new fairy tale characters into the mix, and that's really interesting to me. What's the next one going to be? And how totally different is it going to play out, compared to how you remember it as a child?

**Steve Pearlman:** And I can make an argument for every single one of our characters. I think they are all interesting in their own right. The challenge with any show, as you go into season two and three and beyond, is how do you be truthful to the core of the show, but also, how do you expand *beyond* the core of the show? It's really important to still offer the audience the central conflict, but also keep everything fresh and unpredictable.

# By the Book

ONE OF THE FEW CHARACTERS NOT TO HAVE A CLASSIC STORY ORIGIN (AT LEAST AS FAR AS WE KNOW!), HENRY MILLS IS STILL A PIVOTAL FORCE. IT WAS HIS PLAN TO BRING EMMA TO STORYBROOKE AND HIS KNOWLEDGE OF AND BELIEF IN THE LEATHER-BOUND FAIRY TALE BOOK THAT KICK-STARTED IT ALL. HERE, ACTOR JARED GILMORE TALKS ABOUT PLAYING STORYBROOKE'S LITTLE BOOKWORM...

Words: Tara Bennett

With all of the spells, magic, and dual-character complexities going on in *Once Upon a Time*, it's easy to forget that the heart of the show stems from a brave little boy who just wants to find his true family. Henry Mills is the instigator of all the narrative magic with his stubborn quest to disregard his powerful adoptive mom, Regina Mills (Lana Parrilla), and leave home to bring Emma Swan (Jennifer Morrison) back with him to Storybrooke. Since that fateful day, Henry has seen a whole lot of amazing things and has come to bond with Emma (his biological mom) and his grandparents, Snow White (Ginnifer Goodwin) and Prince Charming (Josh Dallas).

For eleven-and-a-half-year-old Jared Gilmore, playing Henry has been his own fairy tale come true as it allows him to pretend daily with a cast of characters he's loved his whole, young life. Not to mention the fact that Gilmore now also gets to spend most of his year in Vancouver, British Columbia, shooting the hit series on soundstages and in fun locales that are a lot more intriguing than a typical schoolroom. In an exclusive interview, Jared tells us how he adores *Once Upon a Time*, and how it's changed his life.

**Jared, what was it about the *Once Upon a Time* 'Pilot' script that made you interested in playing the character of Henry?**

I think it was because he was convinced that everyone was a fairy tale character from another world. Also, I just love fairy tales so much. I have a twin sister [Taylor], so me and her would always watch the Disney Princess movies so we know about the fairy tale stories.

**Since you're a fairy tale fan, which characters did you hope were going to be in the show?**

The Seven Dwarfs, because I've always loved them. And then I also liked Prince Charming, because he's a cool character.

**In the 'Pilot,' you played Henry with a confident, singular purpose. Did that come easy to you on a big set with lots of actors you had just met?**

It was really cool because I didn't have to get into the part. I felt like me and Henry had a lot in common, so I got into the role pretty easily.

**What do you feel you both have in common?**

Henry and I both like fairy tales. Also, sometimes, because I have a twin sister we disagree about a lot of things. I will try to tell her something is right, but she won't believe me, so it's sort of like the relationship between Emma and Henry.

**How has it been getting to know Jennifer Morrison, who plays Emma?**

When we first met and started acting with one another we clicked, because she's such a nice person. When we're waiting for scenes we just like talking to each other.

"BEFORE HENRY MET EMMA HE SPENT 10 YEARS WITH REGINA, SO I THINK HE DOES CARE FOR HER BECAUSE SHE RAISED HIM."

105

**You have a very different on-screen relationship with Lana Parrilla because your characters have such a difficult mother/son dynamic. Was it hard to get used to real Lana and then mean Regina?**

Lana is just so nice, and so amazing. She is such a nice person, so it's really weird seeing her being so nice when she's not doing a scene, and then when she's on set doing the scene she *is* the Evil Queen. She's so good at it! Her personality can completely change when we're doing a scene together or when she's doing a scene with anyone. She's amazing.

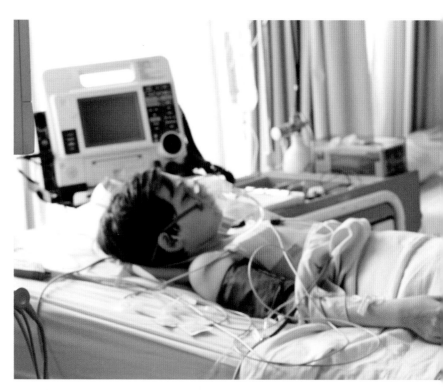

**What was your favorite scene with her?**

I have a couple I really like, but I think my favorite one is when I'm running home in the Cinderella episode ['The Price of Gold']. My shoe falls off and I run in my room. She comes barging into my room and says, "What have I always told you? Don't leave your shoes on the staircase!" I loved that moment. It was so much fun.

**At the end of Season One, did the writers warn you that Henry was going to die, and were you at all worried?**

I didn't worry about anything like that. My mom and the rest of my family were blown away by it. They were like, "Oh my gosh!" and I thought it was a cool thing.

**Was playing dead difficult?**

It was unbelievably hard! At one point, because I was supposed to be dead, they didn't want me to be breathing. I had to hold my breath when we were doing the scene until I was woken up. It was challenging because I move a lot. I move so much even when I'm sleeping; tossing and turning, tossing and turning. It was really hard to stay there completely still.

**Do you ever get bummed out that Henry doesn't get to play in the Fairy Tale Land?**

I wasn't super-depressed about that, because it's really fun in the real world. But the one thing I really wanted to do was have a swordfight in Fairy Tale Land.

"IT'S REALLY WEIRD SEEING LANA BEING SO NICE WHEN SHE'S NOT DOING A SCENE, AND THEN WHEN SHE'S ON SET DOING THE SCENE SHE IS THE EVIL QUEEN. SHE'S SO GOOD AT IT!"

**Well, you got your wish this season!**

Yes!

**Speaking of Season Two, you opened this season calling Regina mom for the first time. Did you ever think Henry would say that?**

I think I knew he would say that. Before Henry met Emma he still spent 10 years with Regina, so I think he does care for her because she raised him.

**Do you think Henry can help her on the path to redemption?**

I think Henry can help her become good. I think he really can if he tries hard enough.

**Has it felt like you were on a different show this year,** while Henry has been living with David waiting for Emma and Mary Margaret to come back?

Yes. It's almost like working with a whole new group of people. Last season I had all my scenes with Emma and Lana. This season I'm doing all my scenes with a whole bunch of people, like Josh Dallas and the Seven Dwarfs.

**You get to work with all your heroes! Are you friends with the other actors now? Not many people get to call the Seven Dwarfs their buddies.**

They are so nice. I have a good relationship with a couple of the dwarfs. We hang out all the time and have fun playing Nerf wars and video games.

**So what has been the highlight of Season Two for you so far?**

My most favorite scene is me and Josh Dallas having a swordfight. It was a really cool scene!

**Did you have to work with the stunt guys to train for that?**

We didn't have a lot of training for the scene, but I have gotten to work with the stunt people a lot more this season. It's taught me a lot.

**What do you think about the new characters showing up?**

I really enjoyed seeing Captain Hook on the show, because I really, really love *Peter Pan*. I've seen the animated one, the real-life one, and when we were younger we went to a play of it that my sister's friend was in.

**Do you have a wish list of any characters you'd like to see?**

My sister and I have always loved *The Little Mermaid*.

**Do you mind having to be away in Vancouver so much now for the show?**

Vancouver is really, really nice. I actually like the climate and the weather here more than I like it in California. I like the cold and can't stand the heat!

**Are you learning any winter sports?**

I haven't been in the snow a lot, but when it snowed in Vancouver I was so happy. I was running around in the snow playing in it. Usually when it rains, I'm always inside, because I can't run around and play in the rain. But when it's snowy, you can't get me inside because I love the snow so much!

**Do people recognize you more now because of the show?**

*Some* people recognize me, not a ton, but the show really has changed my life.

- Jared is one of four actors to have played Don and Betty Draper's son Bobby on the hit series *Mad Men*.
- Other acting roles Jared has had include the Jennifer Lopez movie *The Back-Up Plan*, a recurring role on the medical show *HawthoRNe*, playing "Little Bill O'Reilly" in the satirical series *Talkshow With Spike Feresten*, and the sitcom *Wilfred*, in which he played the child version of Elijah Wood's character.
- Jared has won a Young Artist Award for his role as Henry on *Once Upon a Time*, and a Screen Actor's Guild Award as part of the Outstanding Performance by an Ensemble in a Drama Series category for *Mad Men*.

# Whistle While You Work

WHEN IT COMES TO
MAKING A TV SHOW EPIC,
A FACTOR OF HUGE
NOTE IS THE MUSIC.
CUE MULTI-AWARD-
WINNING COMPOSER
MARK ISHAM.
HE TALKS EXCLUSIVELY
TO US ABOUT HOW HE
CAME TO WORK ON *ONCE
UPON A TIME*, AND HOW
THE SHOW'S FAIRY TALE
ADVENTURES ARE UNLIKE
ANYTHING ELSE HE HAS
SCORED BEFORE...

Words: Paul Terry

111

**W**ith such a broad range of movies in your filmography – from dramas like *Crash* and *Lions For Lambs*, to horror films like *The Mist* and *Blade* – what led you to compose for a fantasy show like *Once Upon a Time*?

**Mark Isham:** I hadn't done television in quite a while, and the head of music for ABC Studios called me up and said, "I've got a script that you might be interested in, to coax you back into television." *[laughs]* So I said, "Okay, I'll read it." Sure enough, I loved it and said that I would love to meet with the guys behind it. I went in to meet with [co-creators] Eddy [Kitsis] and Adam [Horowitz], and it was just like kids in a candy store from the moment we met. They asked me right then and there to do the show, and I said yes. It was very quick, and very easy.

*Once Upon a Time* is so imaginative, and they are so cool and talented, that it was a no-brainer for me. And the other part of it – which is equally important, as it's part of the day-to-day process – is that ABC, especially their music department, are so supportive of the music. They really love music, and they really value it highly. We get an orchestra every week and we're allowed to have fun but also turn out a very high-quality product.

It was a very wise decision for them to [prioritize] that. These are iconic stories, and from the times we have been introduced to these characters in film form, they've been accompanied by an orchestra. From the first Disney presentation 70 years ago, they've always been accompanied by beautiful songs and big orchestral productions, and so we've kept that aesthetic alive. I like to think that it's a big part of the show.

> ## "FROM THE FIRST DISNEY PRESENTATION 70 YEARS AGO, THESE STORIES HAVE ALWAYS BEEN ACCOMPANIED BY BEAUTIFUL SONGS AND BIG ORCHESTRAL PRODUCTIONS, AND SO WE'VE KEPT THAT AESTHETIC ALIVE."

**Were there any previous projects that especially helped you create the musical landscape for *Once Upon a Time*?**

Nothing really *exactly* like *Once,* and I think that's personally one of the reasons why I was so attracted to it – it was a real expansion for me. I've done a lot of dramas, horror films, dark films, some lighter stuff, and in the past few years I've done a number of family films, which are fun. As I have children, I've always wanted to bring my children more into my work. For a long time they would come home from school and I'd have to turn off what I was working on… some of that stuff shouldn't be exposed to a six year-old! *[Laughs]* So this was another opportunity to really invite my younger children into the work I do,

# "I WROTE AN EVIL QUEEN THEME BEFORE I SAW ANYTHING, AND EDDY AND ADAM SENT IT BACK AND SAID, 'YOU KNOW WHAT? SHE'S GONNA BE MORE EVIL THAN THAT!'"

## Collaborations

On top of his solo work (including the Grammy-winning self-titled album, *Mark Isham*), Isham has recorded with some of music's most iconic and popular artists through the years, including Joni Mitchell, The Rolling Stones, Herbie Hancock, Willie Nelson, Chris Isaak, Van Morrison, Sting, Will.i.am, and Bruce Springsteen.

which is very important to me. I think my work in family films was probably my biggest training ground for this, but I really set out to challenge myself. I wanted to develop my own "mini genre" as it were – to bring several elements together that could be done on a weekly basis that hopefully, in a fairly unique way, help define the show.

**Some fans may not be aware of the long and detailed process that goes into creating the score each episode. Could you talk us through the various stages?**

Sure – we start with a script, and we get the first draft that the writers are happy to send out. We may go through five or six drafts, but I don't necessarily read all of them. I certainly read that first one, as I really want to know the gist of the story and where we're headed. For me, of course, it's very important to know if there are any new characters. I've taken a very old fashioned approach with this: we have themes for characters, which is something I've not necessarily done a lot of...

**That's something that's particularly striking – the character cues are very much a strong part of *Once Upon a Time*'s scoring style.**

Absolutely. I find in modern filmmaking, your musical themes want to be more *philosophical* if you will – "betrayal" or "trust" or "the family theme," things like that. You don't necessarily need the *Indiana Jones* "here he is on screen" style of music cue. That's a very much older, traditional style, which I haven't worked in a lot, but I thought that for this show, it would be perfect. So every time there's a new character, we have to write that character's music, so that's really the first thing I look at.

Then we have a rough cut of the editor's cut, to see where they're going. The editor has usually put in some temporary music, to show what their ideas are. I go through that and we discuss that, and we finalize the "spotting." This is where we decide where the music starts and stops in an episode. As we're doing that they're locking the picture, finishing it, and making sure the final edits are all in place. On this show, it's interesting because there are lots of special effects, so we usually have green screens or drawings, like the Ogre – he was just a drawing. So sometimes I call up and say, "I got the drawing... but what is this guy about?"

So then it's time to work. You start writing each piece of music, or "cue." By this point in season two, we have a large library of themes and music. Someone like Rumplestiltskin has a huge collection of music, because he's such a large part of the story. The Evil Queen, of course, has her motif, and I got lucky on that one. I wrote her theme for the Pilot, before we knew where we'd be going, and that's managed to really stand the test of time for her. So we write all of the cues for the episode, then I send off demos to producers, and they sign off on them.

Then it goes into the music system: as the demos are all written electronically on computers, it then gets transcribed off the computer and it goes to an orchestrator, who fully orchestrates all of the parts for the full orchestra. That goes to the copyist, who copies all the parts. Meanwhile, we're building sessions with "click tracks" – these timing clicks make sure everything is timed to the exact second. This means the musicians who play along are exactly in sync to the picture.

We then all convene, usually on Tuesday nights at 7:30pm, and do a three-hour recording session with a full orchestra. We take the recording of the orchestra and whatever electronic elements we do use – although the electronic elements are very disguised, they're used mostly to bolster the adrenaline and drones.

It's then time to mix, which can take a full two days, as there is a *lot* of music and layers. We mix Wednesday to Thursday. They also start their assembly mix, which is called a "dub." It's where they mix the dialogue and music together. That starts on Thursday... so we're chasing them a little bit *[laughs]*. We're done by Thursday afternoon, and then the dub is done by Monday, then it's on the air next Sunday. And then... it starts all over again for the next episode *[laughs]*!

**Have you found that some character cues have come into your head more easily than others? Have some gone through quite a bit of development?**
We've been pretty successful once we got going with them. We did have a little bit of a back and forth with the producers at Pilot stage, because we were learning really, like

"I WANTED TO DEVELOP MY OWN 'MINI GENRE' AS IT WERE – TO BRING SEVERAL ELEMENTS TOGETHER THAT COULD BE DONE ON A WEEKLY BASIS THAT HOPEFULLY, IN A FAIRLY UNIQUE WAY, HELP DEFINE THE SHOW."

## Filmography

MARK ISHAM has more than a hundred film composing credits to his name. Here is a sampling of some of his most famous scores from the past two decades...

*Warrior* (2011)
*The Mist* (2007)
*Lions For Lambs* (2007)
*The Black Dahlia* (2006)
*Eight Below* (2006)
*In Her Shoes* (2005)
*Racing Stripes* (2005)
*Crash* (2004)
*Moonlight Mile* (2002)
*Rules of Engagement* (2000)
*Blade* (1998)
*Fly Away Home* (1996)
*Nell* (1995)
*Quiz Show* (1994)
*A River Runs Through It* (1993)

"How evil is this Evil Queen?" I wrote an Evil Queen theme before I saw anything, and Eddy and Adam sent it back and said, "You know what? She's gonna be more evil than that," and I said, "Oh, okay!" *[laughs]* So, the next time I really amped it up. Of course, I saw how evil she becomes, so it's gotten more dark and twisted since then. It's good that we have a chance every week to embellish and build these themes and give them more depth and substance as we go. I don't think we've had any snafus. That's an observation I made when I first met Eddy and Adam – we just seemed to be on the same page. We seem to not need a lot of translation between our concepts and aesthetics.

I also work with producers Steve [Pearlman] and Brian [Wankum], they're really great. I think one of the things for me – because it is arduous and long hours – is that it's good to have a great team. That's one thing I can say about this show, from the top to the bottom, I love everybody. It's really fun to be with these guys.

**What have you found the most musically challenging aspects of season two so far?**
The Giant in season two was a challenge. How big do you make the music when you have a Giant? We went back and forth on that. I think I overshot it the first time, and then I think we came to a good balance on that.

**One of the most beautiful character cues on the show has to be Snow and Charming's love theme...**
Well, on that note... and I think this is the highest compliment anyone can ever be paid, my 16-year-old son turned to me after hearing that theme for the first time, and said, "Dad. That's the most beautiful piece of music I've ever heard." From a 16-year-old *boy*! *[laughs]* He drives a Camaro and plays football, so it was not the reaction I expected, but it meant the world to me. ❧

Belle
of the
Ball

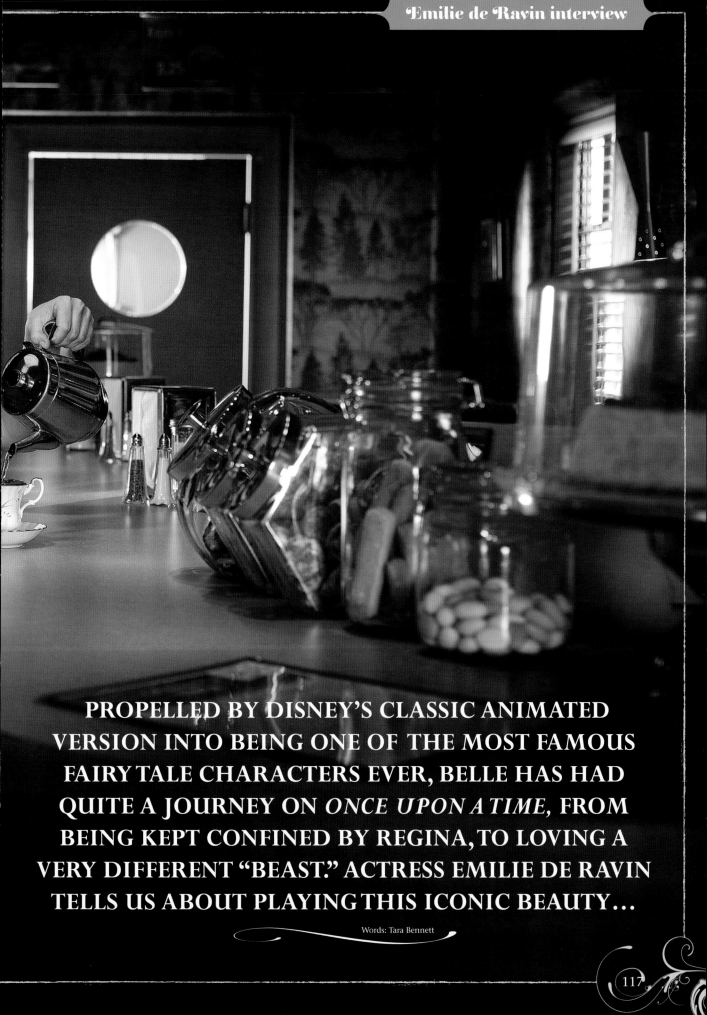

PROPELLED BY DISNEY'S CLASSIC ANIMATED VERSION INTO BEING ONE OF THE MOST FAMOUS FAIRY TALE CHARACTERS EVER, BELLE HAS HAD QUITE A JOURNEY ON *ONCE UPON A TIME,* FROM BEING KEPT CONFINED BY REGINA, TO LOVING A VERY DIFFERENT "BEAST." ACTRESS EMILIE DE RAVIN TELLS US ABOUT PLAYING THIS ICONIC BEAUTY…

Words: Tara Bennett

**A**s the beautiful, smart and compassionate Belle, actress Emilie de Ravin (formerly known as Claire Littleton on ABC's *Lost*) is managing a tricky tightrope with the character. She's both honoring the classic character and the iconic version of her in Disney's animated *Beauty and the Beast*, while also making the *Once Upon a Time* version original and unique.

Belle's "Beast" on the show is Rumplestiltskin/Mr. Gold (Robert Carlyle), and audiences are totally rooting for Belle and the, hopefully, transformative power of her true love for the still wicked cad. Will they live happily ever after? The answer to that is still far, far away but the actress talks to us about how enchanted she is to be playing such an iconic role…

**When you got the call from Eddy Kitsis and Adam Horowitz to take on the part of Belle in 'Skin Deep' did you know much about the series?**
**Emilie de Ravin:** I had heard of the show, but I wasn't familiar with the entire concept. They called about the one episode ['Skin Deep'], but it was just the one episode at that time. It then became this instantly cool thing, because they're fantastic writers. They know how to engage people and write things that make people think, instead of just couch potato viewing.

**They brought you back a month later for 'Dreamy' and then your character got a deeper arc. Did you stay because of your connection with Eddy and Adam thanks to *Lost*, or because of the story?**
Both. It was really just the connection with them and knowing they would write something cool. Belle's an iconic character. I knew I would also be working with Bobby [Robert Carlyle], and I've loved his work for God knows how long.

**How much did you know about the Belle character from the animated films, and was it in any way nerve-wracking bringing the live-action version of her to life?**

"IT'S SO REFRESHING THAT ALL THE WOMEN ON THIS SHOW ARE STRONG IN DIFFERENT WAYS. IT'S SO NICE TO BRING THAT TO A CHARACTER."

## Did You Know?

■ Before becoming an actress, Emilie de Ravin trained as a ballerina.

■ The part of Belle, or the Beauty, has been played by many actresses in different adaptations of the story through the years, including Susan Sarandon, Rebecca De Mornay, Josette Day, Kristin Kreuk, and Vanessa Hudgens, and was voiced by Paige O'Hara in the classic Disney animated version.

■ Emilie de Ravin (Belle) has a pet dog, the similarly-named Bella.

Actually, I didn't really grow up watching those Disney films. I had never seen *Beauty and the Beast*. I knew of the stories and the general inception of the characters from fairy tale books. So no, I didn't feel any of that pressure. I watched the Disney version actually after I shot the initial episode out of curiosity. I'm glad that I made a point of not watching it beforehand, because I didn't want to be influenced by it. But it is funny because people are constantly, probably, comparing how I'm doing it [with the Disney movie], but the writers have done a good thing twisting things around, like having Belle with Rumplestiltskin. It allows for us to not feel the pressure, because it's not a direct comparison.

**After six seasons on *Lost*, you did films like *Remember Me* and *The Chameleon*. Were you happy to be back on TV with *Once Upon a Time*?**
I really couldn't be happier. For me it's not really about whether it's TV or film; more than anything it's about the creative people and all the lovely people you're surrounded with. I'm very lucky to be working with the people that I am, in a great place like Vancouver. [TV can be both] a pro and a con because it gives you the chance to establish the character if it's a successful show, but at the same time you don't want to get bored with a character. But with a show like this, it doesn't really allow you to get bored.

**Does this show feel in any way like *Lost* for you, aside from having the same writing bosses?**

It's cool that it's similar to *Lost* in a sense that I'm playing [different versions of the same character] – Storybrooke Belle and Fairy Tale Land Belle. It's a pretty drastic change between the two, which is fun to play with.

**We have gotten to see Belle in some fantastic costumes inspired by the animated film. Do you have a favorite?**

Basically everything Eduardo [Castro] puts me in! The entire wardrobe department is so creative and so talented. We're very lucky. I've loved everything except the hospital gown, and even that fit nicely! [*Laughs*] But yes, the gold dress and the blue dress are so iconic. Everyone knows what they look like, and they aren't made to be exact representations, but they are absolutely stunning. If you look at the details on the work of any of our costumes from Fairy Tale Land, you think it would take a year to make, but they're whipping them out in three days. It's ridiculous! Every stitch is perfect! However, you don't really eat much on those days though. Eating and a corset make breathing really hard. [*Laughs*] They don't really go together. You're like, "Why does catering smell so good today!"

**The women on *Once* are all very strong, which is rare in any medium. Has that been an unexpected perk of the show?**

Yes, it's a struggle to find strong female characters. It's so refreshing that all the women on this show are strong in different ways. It's so nice to bring that to a character. It's also great for young girls to see that.

**Belle has been through so much because she's so open with her heart. Is her heart a liability, especially when it comes to her complicated romance with Mr. Gold/Rumple?**

There is a certain fragility to her, but that's a first glance perception of Belle. But then if you look into her and spend time with her, you'll find she's one

> "THERE IS A CERTAIN FRAGILITY TO HER, BUT THAT'S A FIRST GLANCE PERCEPTION OF BELLE. BUT THEN IF YOU LOOK INTO HER AND SPEND TIME WITH HER, YOU'LL FIND SHE'S ONE OF THE TOUGHEST CHARACTERS OUT THERE."

of the toughest characters out there. Yes, she's put herself on the line for what she believes in, and that's all that matters. It's not for selfish reasons at all. She's not trying to prove a point to look better, but rather because she actually believes in something. She doesn't care what people think about her, especially in Storybrooke. She doesn't really know anyone, so there's no one she's trying to impress. It's all from a belief in love.

**You get to work with Robert Carlyle as he crafts two very different performances of the same man. Has that been fun for you?**
Yes! If you look at his body of work, it's no surprise that he's doing what he does with this character. He's able to slip on a different hat on a different day and just become that character. I do not envy him the Rumplestiltskin make-up though. I'm very glad I don't have to sit for an hour and a half to get that on my face! [*Laughs*]

**Since Belle's been in Storybrooke and now runs the library, she's opened up more. What are your favorite moments?**
All of them. None of those moments were frivolous because they help tether her physically to a new land. It's nice that her friendships have all developed where everyone can see, like the Ruby relationship, which is very sweet and organic. And all the moments with Gold are specifically important. There's that moment over the hamburger, and leading up to that where she's half-crying and showing that she's not giving up. She's sad when they're arguing and it basically looks like they won't talk again.

**You're discovering Belle's arc as you get the scripts. Have any really surprised you?**
I think most of the scripts [have], which makes me so happy, because there's the balance of craving what you want to know and also enjoying the surprise factor. It's really like viewers watching the next episode actually. Just two days ago I shot the scenes with Bobby after Belle has lost her memory and can't remember who she is because she crossed the town line. I cried reading that scene. It was the

> "I HAVE GIRLS COME UP TO ME AND TELL ME THEY LOVE HOW STRONG BELLE IS AND THAT SHE'S AN INFLUENCE ON THEIR LIFE TO BE STRONG"

biggest shocker moment for me. She's established new friendships and a new life in this new world, and then having it just gone in a second is heartbreaking.

**It must have been so emotional after building Belle into the world of Storybrooke to basically take her back to an almost blank slate?**
She's got nothing to go off of. Everyone else had these really elaborate memories from the curse of who they are, and with her she's got nothing. Spending 28 years in a cell isn't very inspiring to most people, I would imagine. It's a drastic 180 from the caring, compassionate, maternal character that she is to a blank canvas, basically.

I'm so completely involved in my character that I couldn't stop crying when I was reading those scenes. It was terrible! Probably the most iconic image apart from Belle herself is that cup: I throw that cup and when it shatters on the wall it's the most painful image. It's the same when Gold is trying to wake me with true love's kiss. [There's] the split second of believing it's worked and then I'm screaming for him to get away from me. It's so good! It's so delicately dealt with in a tragic way.

**Having lived in Belle's skin for a year now, what are you enjoying most about her or being part of this show?**

In general, the coolest thing I can think of is that so many people know who Belle is, and I'm able to influence the character in a positive way. I have girls come up to me and tell me they love how strong Belle is and that she's an influence on their life to be strong, so that's a very cool thing. It's amazing. It goes a lot further than just being a great acting job.

# Visual Magic

*ONCE UPON A TIME* FEATURES EVERYTHING FROM MAGICAL SPELLS TO FIRE-BREATHING DRAGONS TO GIANT WHALES – A BIG TASK FOR ANY MOVIE BLOCKBUSTER, NEVER MIND A WEEKLY TELEVISION SHOW. FORTUNATELY, *ONCE UPON A TIME* HAS VISUAL EFFECTS MAESTRO ANDREW ORLOFF AND HIS TALENTED TEAM TO CREATE THE MAGIC. HERE HE REVEALS SOME TRICKS OF THE TRADE…

Words: Bryan Cairns

In Fairy Tale Land, Andrew Orloff would be considered a mighty wizard. On numerous occasions he's whipped up buildings out of thin air, conjured curses, transformed humans into supernatural beings and summoned gruesome beasts. In the real world, Orloff is *Once Upon a Time*'s gifted VFX Supervisor who brings digital magic to the enchanting TV series. Now in his second season, Orloff admits creators Adam Horowitz and Eddy Kitsis have pushed the visual effects team to new heights.

"Last season, we thought, 'What else haven't we done?' We did everything from a giant whale that eats a CG character on a CG boat on CG water…" muses Orloff, who owns visual effects company Zoic Studios. "But they found a way to up the ante and keep everybody interested. It's been an amazing experience, an amazing challenge for us. I've been doing this for 20 years and I've never done anything like this. I've been in TV my whole career, in visual effects, and this is by far the most challenging, interesting and collaborative thing I have ever done."

That's a pretty big statement, considering Orloff's impressive track record includes such iconic shows as *Buffy the Vampire Slayer*, *Angel*, *Fringe*, and *True Blood*. However, *Once Upon a Time*'s pure ambition and imagination have proven to be creatively rewarding.

"We weren't expecting the sheer amount of Fairy Tale Land that was going to be dependent on us," says Orloff. "We knew from the pilot that there would be some component of virtual sets, which is when we're in Fairy Tale Land and you see the environment like the war room, where they keep coming back to that scene where they are all at that round table with a big fireplace. We knew that became impractical to build as a set. We also had the wedding scene from the pilot, which was a big ballroom event. We knew we were going to have to create those virtually, and shoot those on a green screen to get it done. We thought that would be something we would come back to on a specialty basis. We spent a lot of time in Storybrooke, we spent a lot of time in practical locations in Fairy Tale Land."

"What we found was as we introduced new characters, and the guys started fleshing out the diversity of what Fairy Tale Land is, we started leaning more on this virtual set methodology to create the scope, the scale, the grandeur, and the fantastical elements that everybody has come to crave and expect from the show," continues Orloff. "Whereas, originally we'd spend one or two days on the green stage from every other episode, what we've ended up doing is a library of over 60 virtual sets and we're spending two to five days on a heavy episode for green screen, just creating the environment of Fairy Tale Land."

There's no denying that *Once Upon a Time*'s production values are superb, but it's a joint effort. Many of those castles, dungeons and surroundings are either digitally enhanced or extended.

To achieve the impossible, Zoic Studios developed its own state-of-the-art technology, dubbed Zeus.

"We started using it on a show we were doing with some of the producers on *V*," explains Orloff. "We've really kicked it up a notch and gone from 1.0 to 3.0 over the last season, just using the technology to really work with the art department, to give pre-viz to everybody. We have an iPad App so you can walk the sets. When you get on the stage, we're shooting two cameras. When people look through the camera, they don't see the green screen. They see what the virtual set is going to look like on stage. That's really important, because when we have the characters acting in those environments, they have to know what it is they're reacting to. To make it look real, they need to be able to walk through doors and the camera needs to be able to dolly around the column. The lighting from the fireplace, that's not really there and has to come from the director of photography. The sheer volume we have to do... We turn the shots around in 15 days. There will be north of 300 shots per episode for us to do at the quality level that all the fans and producers have come to expect."

Viewers originally experienced Orloff's bag of tricks in the Pilot. Once the Dark Curse was activated, one dramatic sequence featured Snow and the Evil Queen caught in a swirling maelstrom of broken glass, smoke, magic, and wind.

"It's interesting because we built that nursery set for the Pilot," reports Orloff. "That was a real set where what we ended up doing was putting the ceiling onto that set. One of the more invisible effects

"I'VE BEEN IN TV MY WHOLE CAREER, IN VISUAL EFFECTS, AND THIS IS BY FAR THE MOST CHALLENGING, INTERESTING AND COLLABORATIVE THING I HAVE EVER DONE."

we'll do is build a CG compound on top of a real set. Our department built that set and since we knew we couldn't destroy the set, much less have the actors in there, we invented a new use of the virtual set technology. Instead of constructing the set in CG from scratch, we went into the real set and had the director of photography light it all up. We then took hundreds of pictures from every conceivable angle and we used a proprietary software we built to re-amalgamate those photos. We used technology that takes a bunch of photographs, puts them together and makes a three-dimensional model out of it. We harnessed publicly available technology to our own means. We took the millions of pictures we shot of the set, put them all together and remade the set from the set photography into a 3-dimensional virtual set."

"For example, when Regina starts the curse, Snow is there, Charming is on the ground and it looks like we're on a 360-degree dolly track, spinning around and around...," continues Orloff. "Well, we're not on a set. We're not on a dolly track. We're on a green screen stage and they are on a turntable. We're spinning the virtual set. When the set explodes, we took a bunch of elements of glass that we had shot and put them on a green screen. The smoke that comes in is all computer-generated. There's a computer-generated version of that set that takes over at that point. It's a dead match to the real set to the point that when we come back to the nursery room in the Pinocchio episode and several other episodes in Season Two, where we see it destroyed, that is the virtual version of that real set."

Another element there's never any shortage of in either realm is smoke. There's black smoke, pink smoke and purple smoke, to name but a few. Luckily, Zoic is well known for designing such signature visuals on television shows.

"My philosophy, from way back in the day, is within the logical construct of what this world is, what's the story behind this?" says Orloff. "How does Regina's magic work? What different types of magic are there? The smoke is a big thing. Sometimes the smoke is a curse. Sometimes it's transformative. Sometimes it turns into a fireball, so we really try and

127

key in based on the function of what the spell is and the person who is using it. Rumplestiltskin smoke is different than Regina smoke. Cora's smoke is different than Regina's smoke, but theirs are closely related. Who is learning from whom? The mythos Adam and Eddy have created gives us an incredible back-story that we can go to. Who taught who how to use this? Magic is so personal in the show and we've got to reinforce that in the visuals."

"Literally, we have charts on our walls about the different types of magic we've done, what color it is, and what the mythology is," elaborates Orloff. "When a new one comes up, we have a discussion. Is it something that is new that we've never seen before? Is it related to another spell we've seen? We built up quite a library of effects we can use to do that. From the pilot on, one of the big things from Adam, Eddy and Mark Mylod, who directed the Pilot and set the visual tone for the whole series, is the magic here was not like TV magic before. It was an elemental force everybody was harnessing. That's why we come to smoke and we come to fire and we come to dirt and wind and water. When somebody wants to pull somebody off a horse, they don't do it like Darth Vader. They ask the trees to reach out with their branches and pull them off the horse. A lot of times when Regina throws a fireball, she pulls the fire out of a fireplace and shapes it in her hand."

Not everyone on *Once Upon a Time* is

flesh and blood, either. The Blue Fairy, for instance, is a combination of actress Keegan Connor Tracy and visual effects. The voice of reason, Jiminy Cricket, is fully computer-generated. And when Geppetto and Pinocchio braved the open waters and were about to be swallowed by the mammoth whale Monstro, they animated the beloved wooden Disney character.

"They really wanted to make him not look like a boy in puppet make-up," explains Orloff. "They had a practical puppet we were matching and they wanted it to look like a puppet had gotten magic in it and come to life. There's no practical way to do that. Besides, there was a safety concern. When we shot that, we were in a 60-foot tank, on a boat that was in there, that we were moving around and blowing in the wind. There is no way to get a child on there, so we had a motion-capture actor do the motions of Pinocchio after we filmed the scene."

Fairy Tale Land is a dangerous place. Wolves, ogres and other creatures roam free. It's up to Orloff and his team to bring these monstrosities to life. One of their biggest undertakings was a pair of dragons in the season-one finale, "A Land Without Magic," especially considering there was plenty of close interaction with the actors.

"When there was a lot of 'dragon mechanics,' there was a lot to deal with," notes Orloff. "There was the way the dragon blows fire, where the fire comes from, how Emma decides she can use the

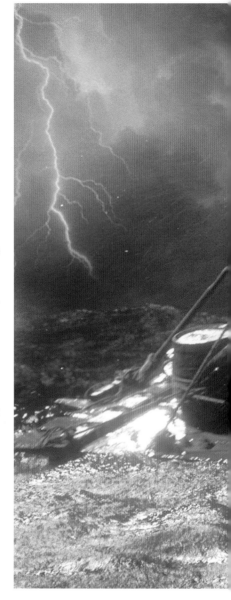

dragon's fire-breathing ability against it to cause it to self-destruct. That was the biggest thing we had to tackle. Like Jiminy, we're working off an existing Disney character. We're looking at dragon-Maleficent from the animated *Sleeping Beauty* and trying to pull the essence of it. Every time we do one of these characters, like Jiminy or Pinocchio, we go back and really look at what the original Disney representation is, because there's so much about the audience's expectation and their relationships with these characters. We want to take the kernel of the source, of what it is about the character that made it cool, and then add something to it for our own world."

Going into Season Two, Orloff

"MY PHILOSOPHY, FROM WAY BACK IN THE DAY, IS WITHIN THE LOGICAL CONSTRUCT OF WHAT THIS WORLD IS, 'WHAT'S THE STORY BEHIND THIS? HOW DOES REGINA'S MAGIC WORK? WHAT DIFFERENT TYPES OF MAGIC ARE THERE?'"

admits one of the major challenges is the increase of computer-animated characters. A prime example is the ominous Wraith, which plagued Regina, David, Prince Philip, Mulan and company in "Broken." Somehow, the ghoul needed to be frightening, but still Sunday-night-family-friendly.

"It's that Halloween-scary that's just the right amount of scary, without being terrifying," says Orloff. "A lot of people asked how we did it. 'Was it motion capture? How did we do the fabric?' It's all hand-animated. Our animators do a great job imbuing these inanimate puppets that live inside the computer with personality. We really spent a lot of time doing that. The technology on how the fabric works and flows was really integral to making that look realistic. We're finding that we're getting into a realm of not every character we see in Season Two is a personality from an existing franchise."

These days, Orloff has been busy with giants, even more wolves and an upcoming fiery demon, to name a few. There are new worlds to map out and fresh faces keep popping up. Amidst the heavy workload, Orloff is hoping a Disney favorite will wash up on the *Once Upon a Time* shores.

"I don't have any idea if they are going to do it, but there have been references to the Little Mermaid," he says. "Ariel is one of the major Disney princesses we haven't seen yet, but I definitely hope we get to do some underwater stuff, because that would be amazing."

Speaking of amazing things, Orloff's long hours and fantastic work haven't gone unnoticed. He's been nominated for multiple visual effects Emmys.

"Part of the way the Emmys for visual effects runs is it is all peer-oriented," concludes Orloff. "It's the people who do the visual effects that give the recognition. In this case, it's a cliché, but to be nominated in that category shows that the visual effects community, especially in television, is really behind what we're doing. I think the show is going to be around for a while, and our stuff is only getting better." ✦

# Seeing Red

## YOU MIGHT HAVE THOUGHT YOU KNEW THE *RED RIDING HOOD* STORY, UNTIL *ONCE UPON A TIME* GAVE THE STORY A TWIST BY MAKING RED THE WOLF! ACTRESS MEGHAN ORY TELLS US ABOUT PLAYING THIS WOLF IN A SASSY WAITRESS'S CLOTHING…

Words: Tara Bennett

For all the angst and drama that tends to permeate Storybrooke and Fairy Tale Land, it's nice to know there's always a respite from the dark, at least when it comes to a fierce firecracker that lights up her screen time in either realm. Red Riding Hood and Ruby are two sides of the same coin, wild women with a penchant for shaking things up with their secrets and resilience.

In Fairy Tale Land, Red's been revealed to be far from the innocent girl of lore hiking through the woods to Grandmother's house. Nope, she's actually the Big Bad Wolf that rears her scary head during the full moon at "Wolf's Time", as a terrifying beast that's only tempered through hard won control and by donning her blood red cape.

In Storybrooke, Ruby is the saucy waitress at Granny's Diner, ready to flirt and happy to earn stares for her eccentric, red-themed outfits. It's the intriguing duality of the woman, played with such energy and spark by actress Meghan Ory, that's made Red/Ruby such a fan favorite. As more of her story unfolds, Ory also brings a sense of honor and independence that makes the cursed woman such a steadying and funny presence in both worlds.

For Canadian native and TV veteran Ory, *Once Upon a Time* was a show that she knew she wanted to be on the second she finished the script. "I had read the Pilot before they started casting any of the roles," she explains, "and I was hooked!"

Given the chance to audition, Ory says Ruby was presented as a dual role. "I read for another part and then Ruby. The first time was [an audition] on tape and then I went in a couple of times, so it was probably a month to get [the part]."

In preparation for the audition and how she would put a spin on Red/Ruby, Ory says, "I did do a lot of research on Red Riding Hood. The description for Red in the Pilot was that she was basically trashy. I thought that was interesting," she chuckles. "I started reading about her and how basically the [original] story is all innuendo, and a cautionary tale for young girls to not be prey for lecherous men. I took that as inspiration for Ruby in the first season. When I asked [creators Eddy and Adam], they told me they sensualized her because of that."

Funnily enough, Ory says she never really got what the scope of her character's arc would be until she was cast and started getting vital details from Kitsis and Horowitz about Red's true nature. "They told me early on where things were going to be going with her later," the actress remembers. "I think around episodes four or five they started giving me little hints and then they told me what was to come in episode 15 ("Red-Handed") which was nice."

In fact, that episode became Ory's favorite from the first season. "[Writer and consulting producer] Jane Espenson wrote that episode, and I think she did a brilliant job. I love the arc of both characters and how they followed each other in the same way in terms of what happens to both

characters. It was so interesting to play them at the same time and see them side-by-side. It was incredible."

Asked if she preferred making choices about how to play Red or Ruby when she was more in the dark about the characters, Ory pauses and mulls, "That's a very good question, because I kind of like both ways. Before, not knowing could be nerve-wracking because you don't know if what you are doing is going in the right direction. You have to just decide on something, which is invigorating and fun because you can't

be wrong if you don't know. It makes for very interesting watching, because everybody is coming at it from a different angle. But I feel there's something that ends up becoming a commonality anyway because you're guessing. It's kind of cool when a guess is actually right. [The writers] do give a lot of hints if you look for them, and I think that's what makes the show so great to watch. The fans are super-fans and they want to delve into the world. It's the same for the actors that if you look for the hints, they're there. But when they tell you

> ## "I HAD READ THE PILOT BEFORE THEY STARTED CASTING ANY OF THE ROLES, AND I WAS HOOKED!"

exactly what's happening that's fun too!"

Another early perk for Ory was the costuming for her characters. She says she quickly fell in love with the vixen-inspired outfits from Ruby's closet. "She's very interesting, because she's gone through pretty crazy costumes in a pretty short amount of time," Ory laughs. "I love it! I always liked Ruby's look. I remember one where I was wearing red pleather thigh-high boots, then a red sash and a red hat. I went in for my fitting for that and it was totally fun!"

## Did You Know?

There have been many versions of the *Red Riding Hood* story through the years, from Charles Perrault's earliest printed version in the 17th Century, through the Brothers Grimm's famous version in the 19th Century and beyond into the present day. The ending to the story has varied over the years – in some versions of the tale, Red Riding Hood and her grandmother are saved by the Woodcutter from the Wolf, while in others they get eaten!

In one version of the story, "The True History of Little Goldenhood," the character wears a golden cloak instead of a red one, which repels the wolf because it's enchanted. On *Once Upon a Time* of course, the enchantment of Red's cloak keeps the wolf within her at bay while she wears it.

Red isn't the first supernatural character Meghan Ory has played – among others, she's played a girl possessed by the spirit of a vampire hunter on *Vampire High*, a rehab patient turned into a vampire on *Sanctuary*, and a Vetala (a kind of Indian ghoul) on *Supernatural*.

Aside from looking incredible, Ory says she's always appreciated that the wardrobe has another meaning too. "I think what's so nice is that her inner turmoil was represented in her outward appearance. The need to make her feel better about herself, which I feel is part of her curse, and what she went through in her Fairy Tale Land life manifested in the real world in the need for attention and approval. Now, she's really integrating

"I FEEL LIKE SHE'S STILL GOT THE DESIRE FOR AFFECTION. BUT I FEEL LIKE WE ALL HAVE THESE TRACES OF OUR CURSED SELVES THAT REMAIN IN SOME WAY."

more into Fairy Tale Red. I feel like she's still got the desire for affection. But I feel like we all have these traces of our cursed selves that remain in some way."

Speaking of post-Curse Storybrooke, the Season Two episodes so far have given Ory the chance to really merge Ruby and Red into one body for the first time, tracking the important traits of both women together in subtle ways. "It's definitely a task that demands your attention," Ory says. "It's all interesting because we're all in a new place. It's interesting looking at what our relationships were with certain characters in Storybrooke versus what they were in Fairy Tale Land. It's interesting looking at the interactions with people and figuring out if you knew them from before, or what was the last interaction you had with them in Storybrooke? It adds a real depth to everything. I also think it's great because you can't be lazy. You have to be vigilant all the time and everyone [on the show] is like that. Maybe that's why people enjoy the show so much, because everybody puts a lot of work into it."

She continues, "In Red's case, she has been through so much in her life and she has so much to atone for that she really wants to help people [in Storybrooke]. I think anytime she can help anyone that's really [what's] most important to her. I think it's really interesting."

Of course a highlight of Season Two so far for Ory was the episode "Child of the Moon" where we met her long-lost wolf mother Anita (Annabeth Gish) and saw Red embrace her dual nature finally as woman and wolf. "Anita brings a lot [to Red's life]," Ory says. "She's a very important person in Red's life, and is there during a time when she needs someone to be there for her. [The episode] definitely was more about how Red is pre-Peter dying, and then how very different she is from the Red going to war with Snow and Charming."

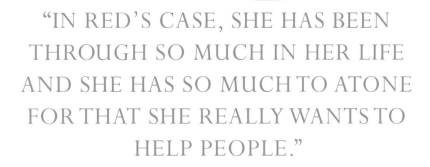

"IN RED'S CASE, SHE HAS BEEN THROUGH SO MUCH IN HER LIFE AND SHE HAS SO MUCH TO ATONE FOR THAT SHE REALLY WANTS TO HELP PEOPLE."

It also solidified the importance of Snow in Red's life, reinforcing their unique bond. "[The writers] took their friendship and expanded it which I am really happy about," Ory enthuses. "One of the things that I love most is how they built that friendship as a pure friendship. You don't see that a lot [with women in fiction] because there's always competition, or animosity or jealousy behind friendships. But with Red and Snow there's a real sense of caring for one another – they've been through stuff together, and they're supporting each other. I love seeing that and them together, and how the writers have brought them together in that way."

It's another reason why Ory says she couldn't wait to get Snow, and Emma, back to Storybrooke. "It's very lonely in Storybrooke without them," she sighs wistfully.

As to Red's future, Ory says she's curious about whether her character can love again after she tragically killed Peter in her wolf guise. "I think Red is very grey because she's been through so much." She continues, "I think she would love to open herself up again to the idea of being loved and trusting herself around someone again, but I don't know if she will be able to. I hope we get to explore that, because I don't know what will happen." ✿

# Impossible Things

LEWIS CARROLL'S WHITE QUEEN SAID SHE COULD BELIEVE SIX IMPOSSIBLE THINGS BEFORE BREAKFAST. AS *ONCE UPON A TIME*'S SPECIAL EFFECTS COORDINATOR, PHIL JONES DOESN'T JUST BELIEVE IMPOSSIBLE THINGS, HE MAKES THEM HAPPEN. HERE HE SHARES SOME SECRETS OF HIS JOB COORDINATING THE CREATION OF EVERYTHING FROM RUNAWAY MINE CARTS TO STORM-TOSSED RAFTS, FROM A PIRATE SHIP TO A GIANT BEANSTALK!

Words: Bryan Cairns

There's never a dull moment on *Once Upon a Time*. One week, special effects coordinator Phil Jones is harnessing Mother Nature, and the next he's erecting a gigantic beanstalk. With credits that include recent incarnations of sci-fi sagas *Battlestar Galactica* and *V*, Jones is used to the hectic TV grind. Nonetheless, *Once Upon a Time*'s bold practical effects soon gave him an amazing new sandbox in which to test his resourcefulness.

"Normally, on other shows, you have standards that you do every week, like wind and smoke," explains Jones. "On this, we have regular stuff we do every week such as atmospheric smoke in the interior sets and atmospheric smoke in the woods. But then every episode, there's one or two big gags that take all your time and energy to somehow put together, and make work, in eight days. You're finishing an episode and then you go right into the next show."

Since the series began, Jones has loaded *Once Upon a Time* with stunning visuals. The Pilot alone crammed in plenty of monumental moments and one dazzling sequence in particular resulted in many, many sleepless nights for Jones.

"We were blowing up the nursery set," he explains. "When the curse comes, they wanted us to blow up the entire room. The room was filled with leaded glass windows. We had to blow them inward, so we had all these air cannons outside the set. We were blowing up the room as an element practically, and then they were going to put the actors back into it. We were blowing candy glass and plexiglass into the plexiglass windows. We had a phantom camera, which has some astronomical [number of] frames per second, so they could slow it down super slow. The problem is when you're running that many frames, you have to cue the camera at the last possible second, or else you'll be sitting there for five minutes, looking at nothing happening before it happens in real time.

"We blew up this entire room, and the camera didn't come on fast enough, so we missed the shot," continues Jones. "It was a good two-or-three-hour set-up too. It was insane. We needed to go again, but we were like, 'But we don't have another one of these fancy doors made out of plexiglass which they had painted by hand.' We actually took the real custom-made leaded glass window and had eight effects people with microscopic tools cutting every piece of lead connecting point. Then we blew it and got it all on high-speed camera. When we all stood around on the day and watched it on playback, it was the most magical thing you could possibly imagine. Every single shard of glass was moving through the frame super slow and it looked like beautiful snow falling, but it was falling horizontally through the frame."

Turnaround for a TV series is crazy quick and it's mind-boggling what's accomplished under such a tight deadline. To keep on top of everything, Jones

The beanstalk, from sketch (bottom) to work-in-progress

frequently requests they put off the filming of various settings or feats until the end of the schedule.

"Things like the beanstalk… there's so many different departments involved in it," says Jones. "For something like that, we get the script and it's like, 'You want to do *what*?' We seriously sit around and look at each other and go, 'Okay, so how are we going to do this? And how are we going to do it in eight days?' Then we get the drawings from the art department and try to conceptualize what it's actually going to look like. It's amazing that when it comes out the other side of the machine, it's so close to, if not exactly, the same as the way it was originally envisioned. For the beanstalk, we built a 25-foot steel structure that we had to transport from the effects shop to the construction shop. We made a steel base for it with casters. Then we put air bags under it, so we could lift it off the ground and it would have some motion when they were climbing on it. Then the carpenters go and build their wooden frame around the outside of it. Then the sculptors go and foam the entire thing. Then the painters go at it. It takes so much time and manpower, and then you see it on screen. There's no way to appreciate the sheer volume of work involved in it. In every episode, there's something like that.

"There was another instance where they wanted a mine cart, in a mine shaft, on wheels, on tracks with one of our main actors [Emilie de Ravin as Belle] bombing around corners and up and down through tunnels," adds Jones. "And we were going to shoot it day three. So we had to build a mine cart and tracks and build all the rail ties and the elevated areas and the steel work for underneath it. Then we had to figure out a way we could actually pull it and push it through the tunnels with an actress in it as fast as we possibly could without it tipping over!

"For the mine cart, we figured the best way to make it stable was to make it ridiculously heavy. It probably weighed 350 pounds down really low to keep the center of gravity low. Then we had a golf cart 50 feet away in the studio with a guy in it, with a radio, pulling the cart through the tunnels blindly, just so we had enough power to move it quickly." ✸

# Ambitious Feats

Jones is also responsible for any bullet heads, explosions, gunfire and cars rolling over. Those visual tricks are rare on *Once Upon a Time*, so it's understandable that what gets his creative juices pumping is "the challenge of the builds and figuring out how to do certain things in very short periods of time.

"It didn't really make it to the cut, but in the sheriff's office in the Season Two premiere ['Broken'], we cabled up and did the cell door ripping off, flying across the room and hitting the wall," says Jones. "In the same scene, we made the desk super-lightweight so the Wraith could flip it and fire it across the room at Charming. Then in that episode, we had some sparks we were doing outside the pawn shop and blowing all the debris down the street and doing interactive debris flying through the air. We had 30 brooms that were pre-burned, and some of them had alcohol or propane on them. Then we had a bunch of the main characters, in a room, with two doors, on a stage, with all of them carrying burning objects. We had them lighting the railing in the room and the Wraith flying around, so we're blowing fans while the actors are carrying flaming brooms."

In Season One's 'The Stranger,' the pressure was on to deliver what Jones considers his most ambitious feat of the series. The script talked about a whale in the middle of the ocean, during a storm, with a live actor and a CG character on a raft. Sure, no problem.

"You're sitting there going, 'How long do we have to do this? And is this a TV show?'" says Jones with a laugh. "We were tapped out for studio space at the time, so we rented a whole other studio, built a 60-foot diameter tank, six feet deep. We filled it up with water, heated the water to 92 degrees and rented some wave-making machines. We had six rudder fans along the side on for lifts. There were rain towers and smoke machines. We re-circulated the water from the pool through the rain towers, so all the rain that was falling was nice and warm. We had water cannons that simulated the waves crashing around them. We built the frame for the raft and made sure that it was going to float and it wasn't going to sink. We then put steel plates on the bottom of the pool to anchor the raft so it wouldn't disappear out of frame. We had an anchor out there for quite a few hours bobbing around in the storm, blasting him with wind and rain and waves, crashing and smashing him. There was a lot of water flying through the air!" ✸

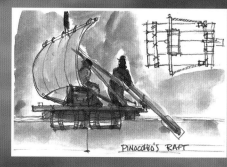

PINOCCHIO'S RAFT

Sketches and production design for the Pinocchio, Geppetto, and Monstro raft sequence

# Ship Shape

From Jones' perspective, every episode is so incredibly different that it's impossible to prepare in advance. Case in point, Hook's pirate ship. When Jones received the script, he simply assumed production would use the pre-existing structure from earlier in the year. Unfortunately, for some reason, it was unavailable, so instead of relying solely on computer animation, they constructed their own vessel.

"In our shop, we built the masts," says Jones. "You're going off drawings of a ship and trying to change it into something you can actually shoot on. Then it's trying to figure out how much of it do we need for this particular episode, and because we're going to have it for awhile, what are we going to need it to do and how much of it are we going to see? Then you look at the budgetary constraints and time frame and you go, 'This is what we think we might be able to give you in the amount of time.'

"So we built the masts, which are 30 feet high," he elaborates. "We made them out of steel and the paint department painted it to look like wood. We had to figure out how to structurally make them sound and weld them to the barge we were going to build the ship on top [of]. We built a truss up on top of that to hang all the ropework off of. We actually got parts from the real boat because they have to do refits on the boats all the time.

"We actually got the yard arms, which are basically telephone poles that hang 30 feet up in the air, and there are two of them. We had to figure out how to hang those up there with sails on them and tons of rope. You have the big boom that goes off the back of the ship and that's all real."

A *Once Upon a Time* episode is roughly 42 minutes. That means despite all the careful planning, preparation and execution, any extra footage lands on the cutting room floor. Even impressive gags aren't immune to being edited out, and Jones admits to being surprised in Season Two when a scene in

'The Doctor' involving Regina, Jefferson and Dr. Whale suffered such a fate.

"They are in Cora's secret room in Leopold's castle and go down into the basement to the secret underground vault," reveals Jones. "They walk into the room that is full of hearts. They are in there, take the heart out and basically trip an alarm in the vault. We had the vault rigged. The gate slammed shut behind them and traps them. Then the walls come in and start to crush them. They take a statuette, throw it on the floor and jam the walls open. Then the ceiling comes down and is about to crush them. It goes from a 15-foot room with 10-foot ceilings to a four-foot room with four-foot ceilings in a very short period of time, with actors in the room. We're out there pushing and we have forklifts moving the walls. Then Regina does a magic spell and they disappear.

"Hopefully," he concludes, "it will end up as a DVD extra."

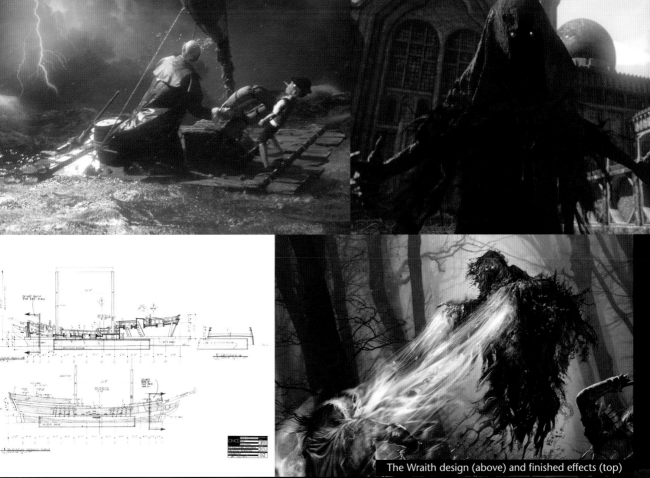

The finished raft sequence, as seen on screen

The *Jolly Roger* designs

The Wraith design (above) and finished effects (top)

# Totally Hooked

SINCE JOINING *ONCE UPON A TIME* AT THE START OF ITS SECOND SEASON, CAPTAIN HOOK HAS BECOME ONE OF THE SHOW'S MOST POPULAR CHARACTERS. BUT IS HOOK AS BAD AS WE ALL THINK HE IS? WE ASK COLIN O'DONOGHUE, THE MAN WHO PLAYS HIM, FOR HIS OPINION...

Words: Jayne Nelson

"**I**t's brilliant!" says Colin O'Donoghue, when asked whether playing a fairy tale character is fun. "I was thinking that on the first day I was on the pirate ship the *Jolly Roger*. I was sailing out and I was in the pirate gear thinking, 'This is crazy!' This is like stuff you dreamed of doing as a child. It's absolutely brilliant to get the opportunity to do it."

Since he first appeared in season two's 'The Crocodile,' Captain Hook has quickly become a major part of *Once Upon a Time*, bringing with him his roguish good looks, his flirtatious relationship with Emma, and his hatred of Rumplestiltskin. When asked about Hook's attempts to charm Emma, O'Donoghue is quite philosophical over whether he'd like to see them explore a romantic relationship in the future.

"What's so interesting about their relationship is that neither of them have the upper hand. This is new to Hook, because he can always see the end game and he can manipulate his way around that. But she gives as good as she gets! They are quite similar characters; they have quite similar backgrounds. She was a thief in her earlier years, and they see a similarity in each other. I think that's what makes that relationship interesting."

While some fans may be rooting for Emma and Hook to get together, others can't see past all the horrible things Hook has done. Most dastardly of these was shooting poor Belle in the back, knocking her over the boundary around Storybrooke and wiping her mind of her love for Rumplestiltskin. But O'Donoghue isn't too shocked at Hook's actions. "Well, first off, he's Captain Hook," he laughs. "People probably shouldn't be too surprised that he has a nasty streak in him! He is considered one of the nasties in literature. He's a nasty piece of work! But the other thing – and this is why I think it's kind of funny when people react saying it's terrible – is that Rumplestiltskin did it to him with Milah. He ripped out Milah's heart and crushed it in front of him. And in fact, Captain Hook didn't actually kill Belle."

Hmm, now that he puts it like that, it doesn't sound too bad in comparison! "At the end of the day with Captain Hook, his thing is that he really did love Milah," O'Donoghue continues. "His overriding objective for the last whatever number of years has been to get revenge on Rumplestiltskin. At whatever that cost is to whomever. That's all he cares about. I think the fact that he uses Belle in that – that's understandable. It's his way of getting back at Rumplestiltskin the way Rumplestiltskin got to him."

It's true that Milah and Hook were in love, and Rumplestiltskin overreacted very badly by killing her. "But he is The Dark One, after all," the actor points out. "It's easy to forget because the characters are so complex – and that's what's so good about the writing on the show – people do forget that these characters are nasty characters, they're evil, they're bad guys!"

We suggest that perhaps if Hook and Rumplestiltskin went to a bar together, had a few drinks and talked things out, maybe they'd be friends. "They would be friends who would happily betray each other," O'Donoghue agrees, laughing.

So how was it filming that scene with Belle, particularly the moment where the car came out of nowhere and hit Hook? "It was an interesting night. That was my stunt double who got hit with the car, and it's weird because when I see him on set he literally looks exactly like me! It was such a big stunt, something like that, you kind of get worried that they're okay. The whole team worked really well. It was an important scene – even more so than the first time they interacted on the boat, this is where he's vulnerable. Every single one of those characters is vulnerable at that point, and it's a very raw, open scene, I think."

Speaking of the boat, O'Donoghue is full of praise for his on-screen vessel.

"They've built a replica of the hull of the ship on a barge, which is more permanent, but there is a proper ship in the first few episodes, the *Lady Washington*. It's amazing because it hardly bobs! You hardly feel the waves at all in it. It was actually the *Interceptor* in *Pirates Of The Caribbean*."

Ah yes, the film series that made pirates cool again. Playing the pirate Captain Hook, does O'Donoghue ever feel a Captain Jack Sparrow influence? "Well, I think people are going to feel that anyway because it's so recent," the actor surmises. "I was conscious that I didn't want him to be like Captain Jack Sparrow. I think he's a little bit more ruthless, manipulative, calculating. I wanted him to be more aware of exactly what he was going to do, methodical and stuff like that. And the eyeliner probably adds to the whole thing as well!"

In addition to the eyeliner, Hook also has a magnificent costume, topped off with a very cool coat. "I have to say, I absolutely love the coat," he admits happily. "When I first tried it on I was amazed. They made it here and it's super-heavy because it's all leather. [Putting on] the costume is when you really feel you're in the character. You have to stand a certain way because of the shape of the waistcoat and all that kind of stuff. I do love that long leather jacket. I'd like to take one home

> "I HAVE TO SAY, I ABSOLUTELY LOVE THE COAT. WHEN I FIRST TRIED IT ON I WAS AMAZED. PUTTING ON THE COSTUME IS WHEN YOU REALLY FEEL YOU'RE IN THE CHARACTER."

with me, but I don't know if I could wear one around town, you know?"

Is there anything we should know about the costume? Does it have any secret pockets, for instance? "No, on the jacket there are no secret pockets. There's a secret pocket in one of the waistcoats, just on the inside. And pockets on the trousers. You probably don't see those because they're so tight..." He laughs. "I don't keep anything in those pockets!"

And of course, no Captain Hook would be complete without his signature item. Is it weird, working with a hook? "You kind of get used to it,"

O'Donoghue says. "He's Captain Hook, so you have to have the hook. It really helps you to feel like you're the character. I've been trying to figure out a good way to use it and what I can use it for, that kind of stuff. The hardest thing was climbing the beanstalk, because I had to climb up one-handed. That was the hardest thing, trying to get used to it. Not having the use of my left hand."

It's not all bad, though. "They're quite useful, hooks," O'Donoghue points out wryly. "You can use them for other things. They can be handy for itches and scratching and punching holes in cartons and stuff."

145

## Emotions and Crocodiles

Fittingly, the first scenes O'Donoghue filmed on *Once Upon a Time* were the ones which included him – as Killian Jones – losing his hand to Rumplestiltskin. "That was Milah getting her heart ripped out and all that stuff, so over the course of it they were all heavy, emotional scenes," he remembers. "I thought it was clever that the writers had written it so that Rumplestiltskin was the Crocodile, with his costume being crocodile leather. It was a great way of doing it! And how they've managed to tie Captain Hook into so many different storylines. I don't know how they do it, they're just really clever."

One example of the writers' cleverness was taking Hook out of Fairy Tale Land and bringing him to Storybrooke – although he largely kept a low profile until he ventured to New York City to make an attempt on Rumplestiltskin's life.

"Tallahassee" was a particularly strong episode for Hook, featuring him and Emma climbing the beanstalk to steal from a giant. Most of the episode involved FX shots and greenscreen – is that a challenge? "You kind of get used to it," the actor reveals. "You get used to knowing exactly where things are and what's going on and you have to trust the director and the FX guys, that they're gonna make it work. And they always do. Some of the set is actually there, and you just go ahead and do it. That's part and parcel of our jobs, to make that believable."

Less FX-heavy were the many scenes with Hook, Mary Margaret, Emma, Mulan, and Aurora, all filmed in the forest. Did he have fun? "I did. There was a good stint there in the woods where I was the only guy, there with all the girls, so I got plenty of advice on shopping and all kinds of stuff that I need to get for my wife! It was nice because the weather was really good at that point, and Vancouver is a stunning place. It's great to get out into the forest and see things you probably would never have gone

## "HE'S CAPTAIN HOOK. PEOPLE PROBABLY SHOULDN'T BE SURPRISED THAT HE HAS A NASTY STREAK IN HIM. HE'S A NASTY PIECE OF WORK!"

to see, and when you get a chance to work there, it's fantastic." He laughs. "I was tied up for most of it, but what are you gonna do? When all the princesses tie you up, you could be doing worse things, you know?"

Many of the actors on *Once Upon a Time* claim to have been fans of their characters all the way from childhood, and this seems to be the case with O'Donoghue and Captain Hook, or at least the story of Peter Pan. "I used to love it when I was a kid," confirms the actor. "I was a big fan of Disney's *Peter Pan* and I was a big fan of *Hook* when it came out. I was about nine or 10, so I loved it."

O'Donoghue has definitely been creating a buzz as Hook. He now has a dedicated Twitter following of fans who have called themselves... wait for it... "Hookers." "Yep, hashtag Hookers," he laughs. "I don't call them that, that was a decision the fans made. I just happened to get a tweet saying 'You should call us Hookers' and I went, 'Well, it's as good a name as any! Okay!' I thought it was a good team name. I don't think people mind. It's nice to be on Twitter and to reply to your fans."

Many of them think that Hook, despite being a bad guy, could be redeemed some day. Does O'Donoghue agree? "Who knows? It'll be interesting to see how he'll develop, because he's still..." He pauses to think, before continuing: "The revenge is still such a big thing and I think that's been driving his life for so long. To see how he could change that, because I think for so long he's been able to use people just to get what he wants. But whether it means he's nice to somebody or whether he's nasty – that's the way he's been working for so long, it'll be interesting to see if it could change. I'm sure it could."

In the meantime, O'Donoghue's simply enjoying playing such an interesting role. "He's great, he's the type of character you can bring so many different elements to. He can be charming, he can be ruthless, caring, funny... He's not tied down by any one specific thing because he's so manipulative. He has a huge arsenal of things to draw from, emotionally, to use people and manipulate people with. It's great to be able to explore all that kind of stuff."

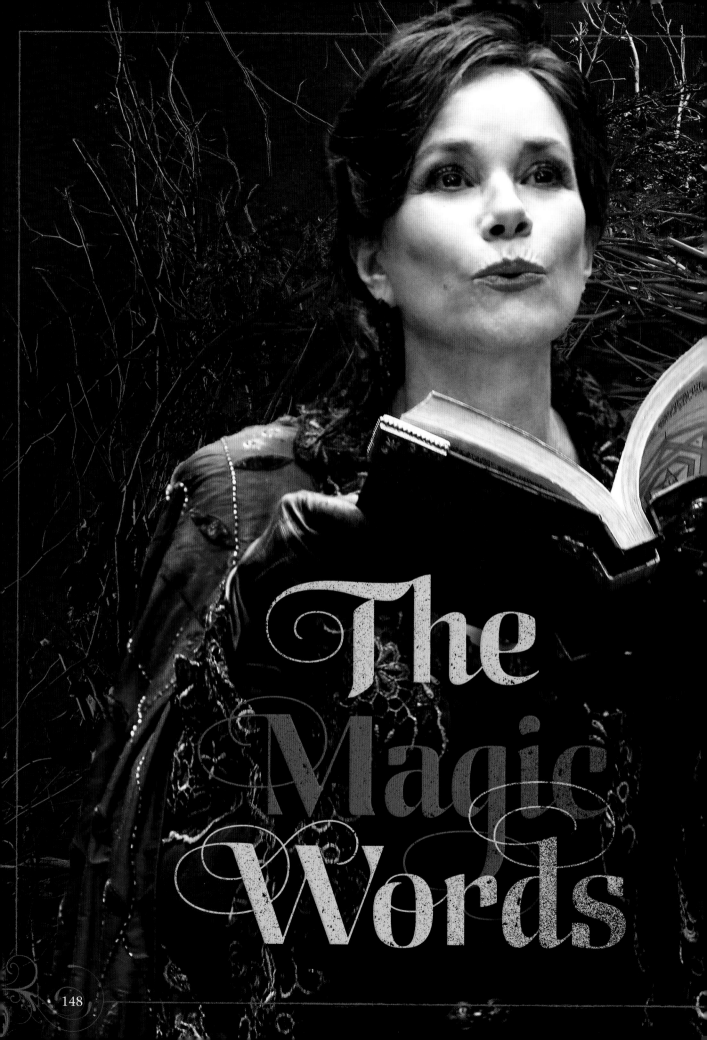

The Magic Words

WE'VE BEEN INVITED BACK TO A TRULY MAGICAL REALM... THE WRITERS' ROOM. IN THE CONCLUDING PART OF OUR MEET THE WRITERS FEATURE, ROBERT HULL AND DANIEL THOMSEN TALK EXCLUSIVELY ABOUT THE EXCITEMENT AND THE CHALLENGES OF CRAFTING *ONCE*'S FANTASTICAL TALES, AND WE CATCH UP AGAIN WITH THEIR FELLOW WRITERS CHRISTINE BOYLAN, ANDREW CHAMBLISS, JANE ESPENSON, IAN GOLDBERG, AND DAVID H. GOODMAN, TO FIND OUT ABOUT THEIR HIGHLIGHTS SO FAR...

Words: Paul Terry

## How did you find yourself in the realm of the *Once Upon a Time* writers' room?

**Daniel Thomsen:** I first met [co-creators] Eddy [Kitsis] and Adam [Horowitz] 10 years ago when I was an assistant/apprentice working in various TV writing offices. I was immediately drawn to their imagination and enthusiasm for art and culture – and not just television! I still have a handwritten list of about 100 'must watch' classic movies they made for me because I didn't go to film school *[laughs]*. As I learned more about the craft of television writing, they read my scripts along the way and gave me invaluable feedback. Once my career was off the ground, I went away and worked on a few TV shows, sold a few pilot scripts,

and then one day I read the news that they'd gotten *Once Upon a Time* on the air at ABC. I asked my agent to get me a meeting, and Eddy and Adam were gracious enough to bring me in. We had a great time discussing the amazing potential of this show they'd created, and the rest is history. I've never worked on a show with this kind of scope and audience reach [before]. It's been an incredibly rewarding experience.

**Robert Hull:** I had met with Eddy and Adam the year before, after reading their amazing pilot. I ended up on *Alcatraz*, and was fortunate enough to work under another amazing writer and former *Lost* Executive Producer, Elizabeth Sarnoff. When that show was canceled, one of the first things I did was ask Liz [Sarnoff] to call Eddy and Adam and demand they meet with me *[laughs]*! They did and somehow I got the job.

**Which of your previous writing experiences have been the most helpful when it comes to crafting *Once* adventures?**

**Robert Hull:** Probably *Alcatraz*, the show I was on before I joined *Once Upon a Time*. A big component of that show was flashbacks, and the co-creator of the show, Elizabeth Sarnoff, worked with Eddy and Adam on *Lost*. I think it was a good introduction to the kind of big-canvas storytelling that the guys are so amazing at.

**Daniel Thomsen:** I wrote for two seasons on *Terminator: The Sarah Connor Chronicles*, and at its core, that show was about a relationship between a mother and a son, and the incredible things we do for family. Here on *Once Upon a Time*, we ground our core relationships in a similar family dynamic. We see the indelible impact that motherhood has had on Regina, and now Emma. We've explored Rumple's complicated relationship with his wife and son. Those relatable dynamics give us the freedom to tell stories with even juicier twists and turns.

**What did you most enjoy about writing for season one?**

> "I'VE NEVER WORKED ON A SHOW WITH THIS KIND OF SCOPE AND AUDIENCE REACH [BEFORE]. IT'S BEEN AN INCREDIBLY REWARDING EXPERIENCE."
>
> — DANIEL THOMSEN

**Daniel Thomsen:** It was so important to make sure that Emma's journey to believing in the curse felt authentic. It couldn't happen too quickly, but we didn't want to test the audience's patience either. In the end, her leap of faith had to be as much about emotion as it was about evidence. We all worked hard on that arc, and I'm particularly proud of how it turned out.

**Robert Hull:** I joined the show [as a writer] for season two, but as a viewer of the first season, it looked as though the episodes were executed with flawless ease.

**Of all the storybook characters that have been given a *Once* remix, which have you enjoyed developing the most and why?**

**Robert Hull:** Definitely Captain Hook. 'The Crocodile'

was the first script I wrote, with co-executive producer David H. Goodman. The spin that the guys and the room came up with was just so incredible. When I went to script, all I kept telling myself was, "It's Captain Hook. Don't screw this up!"

**Daniel Thomsen:** Well, I think I need to give the little-known dwarf of Stealthy his due here. Stealthy, we hardly knew ye!

**What has been the challenge of season two, compared to the tone and storytelling of the first season?**

**Daniel Thomsen:** Balancing three worlds! And it's also been a rewarding challenge to let our baddies from season one – Regina and Rumplestiltskin – share the spotlight with some new evil-doers. I don't think anyone's going to get tired of Captain Hook anytime soon.

**Robert Hull:** Although I wasn't in the writers' room the first season I remember watching the finale and

going, "I can't believe they just did that!" It's really a credit to the guys that they are able to trust their instincts and where the show is telling them to go and then swing for the fences. I think most shows, and most creators, would have played it safe and coasted as long as they could, continuing to do whatever was proven successful in season one. It was a real leap of faith that has paid off huge. Season two just opened everything up. The episodes are incredible.

**What are you looking forward to developing the most as season two powers towards its finale?**

**Daniel Thomsen:** I'm most excited about [Snow finding] herself tempted by the power of dark magic...

**Robert Hull:** The fact that everyone has their memories back and the real and emotional duality our characters are going to have to face and deal with at *every* turn... that's really exciting.

**If you had to choose, which of the episodes – or scenes – you wrote have you enjoyed crafting the most?**

**Ian Goldberg:** There's a lot to get excited about when we sit down to write our episodes. We break our stories as a group, and I'm lucky to work with some of the most imaginative, big-brained, generous writers in television. I also feel very fortunate to have been paired up with Andrew Chambliss. We had a lot of fun working on episodes together in the first season. Of those, yeah, I'd have to say 'The Stranger' is probably my personal favorite, because it allowed us to solve a mystery the audience had been teased with the entire season, by telling the story of Pinocchio. The moment when Emma touches the tree and doesn't believe – no matter how badly August wants her to – breaks my heart every time I watch it. I'm very proud of how that episode turned out.

**Andrew Chambliss:** 'The Shepherd' was fun to write because we got to reinvent Charming's back-story. And the episode contained the first dragon fight I ever wrote in my career. I don't think you ever forget your first dragon fight! My favorite thing about writing 'The Fruit Of The Poisonous Tree' was writing a story where a Genie actually falls victim to his own wishes. It was also nice to take a character

> "THE FACT THAT EVERYONE HAS THEIR MEMORIES BACK AND THE REAL AND EMOTIONAL DUALITY OUR CHARACTERS ARE GOING TO HAVE TO FACE AND DEAL WITH AT EVERY TURN… THAT'S REALLY EXCITING."
>
> – ROBERT HULL

# Family Matters

*Once* writers CHRISTINE BOYLAN, ANDREW CHAMBLISS, JANE ESPENSON, IAN GOLDBERG, DAVID H. GOODMAN, ROBERT HULL, and DANIEL THOMSEN reveal which relationships on the show they get asked the most about by their family and friends…

**Ian Goldberg:** By far, Belle and Rumplestiltskin, aka "RumBelle." People just love that relationship, and rightly so.

**Andrew Chambliss:** I definitely get asked most about Belle and Rumplestiltskin. I think their relationship is a favorite because Belle is one of the few characters who sees Rumplestiltskin/Mr. Gold in the same way that the audience does. So few characters know or actually get to see the side of Rumple that is caring and loving. But we do, and so does Belle. Plus, Belle is one of the only people who understands why Rumple is the man he is – because he's driven by the pain of losing his son. It's a complicated relationship, and I think that's why people are so invested in it.

**Christine Boylan:** RumBelle is popular with my family too. But Regina, and her doomed love with Daniel, is also a big one. I don't think anyone anticipated seeing that vulnerability in the Evil Queen before 'The Stable Boy.' And, of course, Jefferson and Grace – there's no way not to root for that reunion between father and daughter.

**Daniel Thomsen:** Although we didn't get to see much of him in season one, I found that a lot of people were obsessed with the mystery of Dr. Whale's identity. And now that we know the good doctor's back-story, I've been asked some interesting questions about whether there's a particular character in Storybrooke who might have some lasting chemistry with Whale. I love the speculation, because Whale is one of my favorite characters.

**Jane Espenson:** Rumple and Belle, I'd say. I happened to write two episodes that had Rumple stories in them. Writing 'Skin Deep,' our version of *Beauty And The Beast*, was one of the most fun scriptwriting experiences of my career.

**Robert Hull:** What I think is a real testament to the show is that whomever I get asked about keeps changing as we keep changing things up. What's great about *Once Upon a Time* is that even when we shake it up, and take characters in different and unexpected new directions, we always know Eddy and Adam are there as the gatekeepers. They love these characters as much as the fans do and always have their 'True North' in mind.

**David H. Goodman:** My kids are constantly asking me about Rumple/Mr. Gold and the price of magic. I'll be at the dinner table and one of them will do their best Rumple voice and declare that, "Eating beans comes with a price."

like the Magic Mirror and give him human wants and desires. "Heart Of Darkness" was fun just because we got to write Snow White in such an unconventional way, and ask the question, "Could she ever become as dark as the Evil Queen?" 'The Stranger' was exciting because it pushed the mythology of the show forward so much, even if Emma refused to believe the story August told her about coming through the tree with her. Plus, the episode contained the first whale attack I ever wrote in my career, which – like a first dragon fight – is pretty unforgettable.

**Christine Boylan:** Emma's backstory in 'Tallahassee' was such a blast to write – two kids in love in the real world seemed like such an intimate story set against this huge backdrop of epic fairy tale happenings, of which Emma had no idea she was an integral part. That sort of simplicity wrapped in complexity excites me to no end. Also, Emma stealing a car the old school way. Lots of fun to write, and Jennifer Morrison made it look just right.

**Jane Espenson:** I love that this show "goes there." We're willing to make the big turn, do the big reveals, take on characters and do something a little daring now and then. I love 'Red-Handed' because we had Ruby, one of the good guys, with a back-story where she killed and ate her boyfriend! And Jiminy Cricket's past is not without guilt, for what he did to Geppetto's parents. And doesn't that just make perfect sense for a conscience? I love that we go for it.

**Daniel Thomsen:** More than any other show on television, we have an opportunity each week to tell a self-contained, truly emotional story that helps inform the serialized mystery of what's going on with Regina, Rumple, and the curse. Getting that insight into a given character each week and then seeing how it informs their present-day actions is absolutely delightful, from a writing point of view.

**David H. Goodman:** There are too many to choose from. From amazing emotional scenes to sword fights, to magic. There's honestly nothing we're not allowed to do. There are times in the Writers' Room where someone will pitch a story and we'll all just giggle because it sounds so crazy. Like, "Pinocchio is in our world, and has to convince Emma she's the savior so she can save a bunch of fairy tale characters?!" It's just so insane, but it's also amazing. I have one of the best jobs in the world, and I couldn't be more thankful for it.

**Robert Hull:** What excites me not just about the episodes I write, but the show in general, is getting to play around in this amazing world that [co-creators]

"I LOVE THAT THIS SHOW 'GOES THERE.' WE'RE WILLING TO MAKE THE BIG TURN, DO THE BIG REVEALS, TAKE ON OUT-SIZED CHARACTERS AND DO SOMETHING A LITTLE DARING NOW AND THEN." – JANE ESPENSON

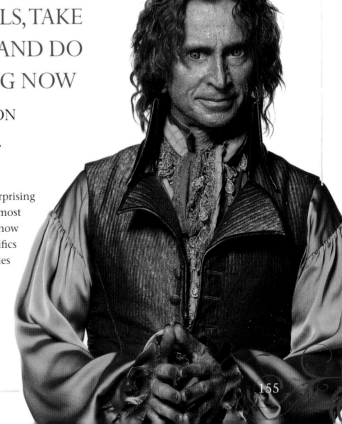

Eddy [Kitsis] and Adam [Horowitz] have created. Getting to explore these iconic characters that I grew up with and then trying to find something new. That being said, the guys have such an immense respect for who these characters are at their core. It's never about retelling a fairy tale or spinning a character just for the sake of doing it. It's about looking at what was already there and digging deeper. Finding the surprising intersections. I doubt most people watching the show remember all the specifics of the original fairy tales we tackle, but I bet they'd be able to tell if we weren't being true to them, which I think is key. ✿

# Season Two
# The Episodes

Words: Chad Ross and Tara Bennett

THE DARK CURSE HAS
BEEN BROKEN AND NOT
ONLY DO STORYBROOKE'S
RESIDENTS REMEMBER
THEIR PAST LIVES, BUT
MAGIC HAS COME TO
TOWN – AND ALONG WITH
IT NEW CHARACTERS LIKE
CAPTAIN HOOK AND TINY
THE GIANT. JOIN US AS
WE WALK THROUGH ALL
THE EPISODES OF SEASON
TWO…

# 2.01 'Broken'

**MR. GOLD:** "MAGIC IS DIFFERENT HERE, DEARIE."
**REGINA:** "I NOTICED."

We open on New York City, where a mysterious man returns to his apartment to find a pigeon on his window sill, delivering a postcard of Storybrooke with a single word, "Broken," on the back. We are left to wonder: who is this man and what is his relationship to our friends in Maine?

Back in Storybrooke, the residents – who now remember their pasts – begin to reconnect. Emma is reunited with her parents Snow White and Prince Charming. Mr. Gold is reunited with Belle, and discovers Regina had kept her hidden from him all these years. Belle begs Mr. Gold not to give in to evil and kill Regina for what the Evil Queen did to her.

In Fairy Tale Land we meet the handsome Prince Philip, the warrior Mulan, and the sleeping princess, Aurora, who Philip must awaken with a kiss. But soon after, a Wraith attacks, and Philip drives it away by taking its magical talisman – an object that will mark anyone who holds it in his or her bare hand, and cause the Wraith to consume their soul. Unbeknownst to Mulan and Aurora, Philip is marked. And back in Storybrooke, Mr.

Gold seems to have possession of an identical-looking talisman...

Meanwhile, the townspeople, led by Dr. Whale, confront Regina – who discovers, when she tries to use magic, that it doesn't work quite the same way in Storybrooke. Just as the mob is about to attack her, Emma, David, Mary Margaret and Henry defuse the situation, and Emma locks Regina in a police cell for her own safety. When Regina's left alone, Mr. Gold visits and presses the talisman to her hand, summoning the Wraith. When Emma, Mary Margaret, and David discover what he's done, they hatch a plan to send the Wraith to Fairy Tale Land with the help of Jefferson's hat – but Regina is unable to harness its magic until Emma touches her, kick-starting the portal. The Wraith is sucked in – and so is Emma. Mary Margaret, refusing to lose her daughter once again, jumps in after her and it closes before David can join them.

Back in Fairy Tale Land, the Wraith comes for Philip, who sacrifices himself to save Aurora and Mulan – who we've come to discover also loves the handsome prince. The women lay Philip on the dais where Aurora slept, but are distracted by a noise. Digging in the nearby rubble, they find an unconscious Emma and Mary Margaret and hold them responsible for bringing the Wraith that killed their prince...

## INTRODUCING:
We meet several new characters in this episode, notably Aurora (Sarah Bolger), Prince Philip (Julian Morris) and Mulan (Jamie Chung). Plus, we see the mysterious man (Michael Raymond-James) in modern-day New York City, about whom more will be revealed...

## ONCE UPON A TIME...
This is the first time we see *present-day* Fairy Tale Land, rather than a pre-curse flashback.

## DID YOU NOTICE?
The message on the postcard the mysterious man receives, "Broken," is the same as the episode title.

Henry magic – but he says he doesn't want to become like her.

At the town line, David and Ruby head off a crowd of scared townspeople trying to leave. David gives an inspiring speech, saying he can understand that they might want to lose their bad Fairy Tale Land memories, but that it's the two sides of them – their Fairy Tale Land and Storybrooke counterparts – that make them who they are. They are both. He promises to protect them if they stay in Storybrooke. He then goes to Regina's house and bursts in. She tells Henry he can leave, as she can't force him to love her and that all she wants is to redeem herself. David asks Regina if the Enchanted Forest still exists, and she confirms that it does. The town finds its equilibrium, while the Dwarfs start to mine fairy dust.

Meanwhile, in Fairy Tale Land, Emma and Mary Margaret are taken as prisoners of Mulan and Aurora to an encampment. Emma and the unconscious Mary Margaret are thrown into a pit. A woman in the shadows tells Emma she's a friend. She steps into the light, and we see it's Cora!

# 2.02 'We Are Both'

**REGINA: "I DON'T WANT THIS LIFE. I WANT TO BE FREE!" CORA: "POWER *IS* FREEDOM."**

t the Storybrooke town line, the Seven Dwarfs test what happens when someone crosses the line, and discover that it erases all memories of Fairy Tale Land and who they were there. Meanwhile, when David confronts Regina about Emma and Mary Margaret's disappearance through the magic hat's portal, she warns him that when she gets her magic back, she'll get Henry back too.

David takes charge amid the growing disorder in the town and becomes acting Sheriff. Regina tries to use magic, with no success, and storms off to see Mr. Gold.

She takes a spellbook from him, but not before he tells her she's becoming like her mother, Cora – the last thing she wants to hear. Using the spellbook, however, Regina gets her magic back.

Mr. Gold prepares to try and leave town to look for his son, but is enraged when he learns he can't cross the Storybrooke line without losing his memories. When David comes to him for help, he gives David a potion to lead him to what he's looking for. Using the potion on the magic hat, David finds Jefferson trapped in a car wreck. He tries to get Jefferson to help him, but besides telling David that Emma and Mary Margaret are in the Enchanted Forest, he says he can't. Meanwhile, Regina arrives at a town meeting and uses her newly regained magic to exert her authority. Henry agrees to go with her to protect the townspeople. When he tries to escape from Regina's mansion, she stops him with one of her spells and offers to teach

# 2.03 'Lady of the Lake'

**KING GEORGE:** "FAMILY IS EVERYTHING MY DEAR. LOSING ALL HOPE OF HAVING ONE... THERE IS NO GREATER MISERY."

In present day Fairy Tale Land, Cora surprises Emma by telling her that she's Regina's mother. When Mary Margaret awakens, she warns Emma to stay away from Cora. The two are taken to see the camp's leader – Lancelot, who Mary Margaret greets as an old friend. Mulan and Aurora are shocked, as they still hold Emma and Mary Margaret responsible for the loss of their love, Philip. Snow tells Lancelot she knows of another portal home to Storybrooke – the wardrobe in her old castle – and sets out to find it with Mulan, but Aurora follows them, and attacks Mary Margaret for bringing the Wraith that killed Philip. Out of her element in Fairy Tale Land, Emma fires her gun, not realizing the noise will attract ogres – and when one appears and attacks them, Mary Margaret shows off her warrior skills and kills it with a single arrow! The four women continue as a group to the castle.

In Storybrooke, Henry talks to Jefferson and persuades him to seek out his daughter. Jefferson lets slip that Regina has a hidden vault in Storybrooke which might have something that could help bring Emma and Mary Margaret back, so Henry tricks Regina into a fake meeting so he can steal her keys. Henry gets into the vault, but opens a box and is menaced by snakes, until David arrives and saves him.

At the castle, Emma and Mary Margaret find the wardrobe, but are surprised by Lancelot's appearance. Emma realizes that he isn't who he seems – that Cora used magic to take on his appearance and pose as their friend! The women fight, and when Cora reveals that she wants to get to Storybrooke herself, Emma burns the wardrobe to stop her. Mulan prevents Cora from killing them, but she escapes using magic. Emma's glad they stopped Cora, but sad that they lost their chance of getting home and, by being in the ruins of this castle with her mother, realizes Snow gave up everything to ensure Emma escaped the curse. Once they've gone, Cora reappears and collects the wardrobe's ashes.

Back in Storybrooke, Jefferson reunites with his daughter, while David finds Henry and gives him some wooden swords so he can teach him to be a knight. As grandfather and grandson bond, they're watched by King George/Albert Spencer...

# 2.04 'The Crocodile'

**MR. GOLD:** "MAGIC HAS BECOME A CRUTCH THAT I CAN'T WALK WITHOUT."

Belle is troubled by dreams that Mr. Gold is still the Dark One, and later finds him actually practicing magic in Storybrooke. She confronts him and tells him it's courage he needs, not power – and leaves. She goes to Granny's, and Ruby suggests that, as a book-lover, she re-open the library. When Belle goes to check out the library, she is kidnapped by a man wearing a red cap.

Gold enlists acting Sheriff David's help to find Belle, and we learn that she was kidnapped on her father Moe's orders, who has learned that she's been staying with Gold willingly. Meanwhile Ruby helps track Belle to Moe's shop. Spotting mine dust on Moe's hands, David realizes he plans to send Belle over the line in the mines under Storybrooke so she'll forget Gold! David, Gold and Ruby find Belle in the nick of time, and Gold saves her with magic. Unhappy with both of them, Belle tells Gold and Moe that neither of them gets to decide what she feels.

Later, Belle receives a key to the library in a box, and Gold tells her that the library is hers now. Gold confesses that he brought magic to Storybrooke and that he uses it as a crutch, and a sympathetic Belle makes a tentative date to meet him. Just when we think Gold has turned a corner, we find him interrogating the red-capped man, who turns out to be William Smee, from Captain Hook's crew!

## INTRODUCING:

We meet Lancelot (Sinqua Walls), who serves King George, before aiding Snow and Charming. In present-day Fairy Tale Land he appears to be an ally, only to turn out to be someone else entirely…

## ONCE UPON A TIME…

In Fairy Tale Land past, Snow is captured by Lancelot and taken to King George, who tricks her into drinking some cursed water that makes her infertile, before releasing her. Charming's mother, Ruth, is mortally wounded by George's men, so Charming, Snow and a repentant Lancelot take Ruth to the enchanted Lake Nostos to heal her. At the lake, they find only a tiny amount of water

left, and Ruth tricks Snow into drinking it, sacrificing herself to heal Snow's infertility. Charming and Snow ask Lancelot to perform a wedding service, so Ruth can see them marry before she dies. Using an enchanted necklace Ruth gave them that can predict the sex of a future baby, Snow learns they will have a daughter.

## DID YOU NOTICE?

At the lake, Lancelot says the words "God in his mercy, lend her grace," a quotation from the poem The Lady Of Shallott by Alfred, Lord Tennyson. In the poem, the Lady Of Shallott is cursed not to be able to look at Lancelot directly, but is unable to resist, and suffers for her curiosity.

## INTRODUCING:

In this episode, we meet Rumplestiltskin's former dissatisfied wife in Fairy Tale Land, Milah (Rachel Shelley), as well as the charming and roguishly handsome pirate Killian Jones (Colin O'Donoghue) who, as Captain Hook, will go on to become one of Season Two's major villains…

## ONCE UPON A TIME…

We learn more about Rumplestiltskin's past, and how his wife Milah left him for the handsome pirate Killian Jones, as she was ashamed of her cowardly husband. After fearfully backing down from a duel with Jones while a mere mortal, Rumplestiltskin

insists on a rematch once he's acquired the Dark One's magic. Milah stops the fight, tempting Rumplestiltskin with a powerful magic bean, but when she reveals that she never loved him, he rips out his wife's heart and crushes it! To try to get the bean, Rumplestiltskin cuts off Jones' clenched hand – but the bean has disappeared. Later, with a hook in place of his severed hand, Jones pledges vengeance and uses the bean to open a portal to a world where he can await his revenge – Neverland!

## DID YOU NOTICE?

Smee is always seen wearing a bright red beanie, a nod to his character's iconic hat in Disney's animated version of Peter Pan.

# 2.05 'The Doctor'

REGINA: "I WANT TRUE HAPPINESS."
RUMPLESTILTSKIN: "THEN FIND IT ELSEWHERE, DEARIE."

**R**eturning to the Safe Haven after failing in their quest to use the wardrobe portal, Emma, Mary Margaret, Mulan and Aurora find the refugees have been massacred, their hearts ripped out! However, they discover one survivor – Hook, pretending to be a scared refugee. They question him, but Emma soon realizes he's lying.

In Storybrooke, Dr. Whale approaches David and asks if it's true that Fairy Tale Land still exists, and whether other lands do too. Meanwhile, Regina goes to Archie for counseling – she wants to give up magic and redeem herself in order to win Henry back. Whale barges in and demands Regina send him back to his world and his brother, but she tells him that she can't. Regina then goes to her family mausoleum, only to find Daniel's body missing, and storms out. Regina looks for Whale and finds him at the hospital with his arm severed. He says he tried to bring Daniel back to life, but he came back as a monster! David finds out about Daniel from Regina, and realizes that Daniel will head for the last place he saw Regina: the stables… where Henry is spending time with his new horse. Henry is knocked over by his spooked horse, and sees Daniel approaching to attack him. David arrives with Regina and urges her to use magic to stop him, but she doesn't want to give up on Daniel once and for all – she sees a glimmer of the man she loved in this monster before he turns on her and attacks. With no other course of action available, Regina must use magic to turn the man she loves into dust.

Regina goes to see Archie and confesses that she used magic, while Whale goes to see Gold. Gold agrees to reattach Whale's severed arm on condition that he admits that he needs magic: an acknowledgment of great consequences as we've come to learn that Whale's other persona is a man rooted in science with little belief in magic. Whale grudgingly does so, and his arm is reattached.

Back in present-day Fairy Tale Land, Emma and the others tie Hook to a tree and make a noise so ogres will come for him. As the ogres approach, Hook tells them he'll help them find the enchanted compass that Cora is searching for which will enable them to get to Storybrooke. Hook leads them to a beanstalk, saying that the compass is at the top… along with a giant!

For the first time we meet Dr. Whale's true self, Dr. Victor Frankenstein, plus his loyal assistant, Igor (Yurij Kis).

## ONCE UPON A TIME...

Regina trains in magic with Rumplestiltskin, but she refuses to kill. We learn that she has kept Daniel preserved in an enchanted casket, and asks Rumplestiltskin if he can teach her to bring back the dead, but he says no. However, Jefferson introduces her to a man who can, known as The Doctor. Examining Daniel's body, the Doctor says he needs an enchanted heart, so Regina gives him one from Cora's vault. The Doctor implants the heart in Daniel, but it doesn't work. Regina returns to Rumplestiltskin to find him training her replacement; heartbroken and angry, she mercilessly rips out the woman's heart. Regina's back in training! Unbeknownst to her, The Doctor meets with Rumplestiltskin and Jefferson, his secret accomplices. Rumplestiltskin is happy that Regina's heartbroken, and the Doctor's happy that he got to keep the enchanted heart – he never really used it on Daniel, as he was saving it for himself. Back in his own land, the Doctor implants the heart in a body under a sheet – his brother. As the body starts to move, The Doctor's assistant congratulates him, calling him Dr. Frankenstein...

## DID YOU NOTICE?

The final scene shot in black and white is a clear allusion to the classic 1930s black and white *Frankenstein* movies. The director of the first two movies, *Frankenstein* and *Bride of Frankenstein*, James Whale, also inspired the name of Victor Frankenstein's Storybrooke identity, Dr. Whale.

# 2.06 'Tallahassee'

**AUGUST:** "I WAS TASKED WITH KEEPING HER ON TRACK AND YOU, MY FRIEND, JUST GOT CAUGHT IN THE CROSSFIRE."

In present-day Fairy Tale Land, Hook leads Emma, Mary Margaret, Mulan and Aurora to the beanstalk and explains that although Jack the Giant Killer murdered most of the giants, there's one left – and that he only has magic enough for two of them to safely climb to the top. Emma persuades the others that she should go and makes Mulan promise that she'll cut down the beanstalk if Emma's not back in ten hours. Emma and Hook climb while engaging in witty repartee, which seems more than a little flirtatious – at least on Hook's part!

Aurora says that she'll take first watch with Mary Margaret – due to previously being under the sleeping curse, she has trouble sleeping and suffers awful nightmares, so she's reluctant to sleep. Mary Margaret assures her that she's been through it too, and that she'll watch over Aurora. When she finally falls asleep, Aurora dreams about being trapped in a burning room, with someone mysterious watching her...

At the top of the beanstalk, Emma and Hook attract the attention of the Giant and put him to sleep with powdered poppy. They search for the compass, but the Giant awakens and Hook becomes trapped under some rubble he leaves in his wake. After escaping the grip of the Giant, Emma activates a booby trap, leaving him stuck under a cage! She finds Jack the Giant Killer's poisoned sword and threatens the Giant until he gives her the compass. He tells Emma that he's not the bad guy and that humans murdered his people. Emma can tell he's speaking the truth, and spares him. The Giant bursts out of the cage and to her surprise, shows Emma a way out. She says that he still owes her, and gets him to release Hook too. However, Emma manacles Hook to a wall, saying that she can't trust him, and leaves. With the ten hours up, Mulan starts to cut down the beanstalk, but Snow fights to stop her before Emma appears.

In Storybrooke, Henry awakens from a nightmare, describing it to David in the same terms as Aurora described hers...

# 2.07 'Child of the Moon'

**ANITA:** "HUMANS MAKE US SEEM THAT WE ARE THE MONSTERS. YOU ONLY BECOME ONE WHEN YOU START BELIEVING IN IT."

## INTRODUCING:
The mysterious man we saw in the series opener is identified as Neal Cassidy (Michael Raymond-James), Emma's ex and Henry's father. We also meet the Giant (Jorge Garcia), whose name we'll discover later…

## ONCE UPON A TIME…
For the first time, this episode's flashback only takes place in the Land Without Magic, not Fairy Tale Land. We see Emma meet the roguish Neal Cassidy when she steals his car, not realizing he'd stolen it himself. The two fall in love and embark on a life of petty crime. When Neal sees a "Wanted" poster of himself, because he stole some watches and stashed them in a locker, he decides he'll have to escape to Canada. Emma offers to retrieve the watches, so they can buy new identities and move to Tallahassee, a place they've chosen at random. After Emma returns with the watches Neal says he'll sell them, but puts one on Emma's wrist as a gift before he leaves. On his way, Neal's accosted by a man who turns out to be August. August tells him that Neal's keeping Emma from her destiny, and that he must let her go, showing him something hidden in a box that convinces Neal to disappear without ever seeing Emma again. As she waits for Neal, Emma is arrested by a cop who sees the stolen watch on her wrist.

Some time later, up in Canada, Neal gives August some money and the keys to the car for Emma once she's out of prison. August tells Neal he'll send him a postcard when Emma's broken the curse. In prison, Emma learns she's pregnant…

## DID YOU NOTICE?
When Emma and Neal rob the convenience store, Neal is nearly caught stealing an Apollo bar. This fictitious snack made frequent appearances on *Lost*, and has popped up in *Once Upon a Time* on a few occasions as well.

The Dwarfs find fairy dust in Storybrooke's mines, and are excited to think that with Jefferson's hat, they can use it to bring Emma and Mary Margaret back. At the diner David is confronted by Albert Spencer (aka his Fairy Tale Land adopted father, King George), who threatens to finally bring him down in this land and expose him for the fraud that he is. Ruby is asked out by the mechanic Billy, but turns him down. In the basement, it becomes clear why – Granny has made a cage to hold Ruby's wolf form for the impending full moon, as Ruby doesn't have her red cloak. The next morning, however, Granny finds that Ruby has escaped the cage in the night! And even worse, David finds Billy ripped in two; Ruby is terrified that she is responsible.

Henry wakes up from another nightmare about the fiery room, this time with a burn on his arm. Regina takes him to see Mr. Gold, who explains that because he was once under the sleeping curse, Henry goes to the Netherworld during his nightmares. Gold gives Henry a pendant to help him control the flames there.

David locks Ruby in a cell for protection, while Spencer whips up public opinion against her. Spencer assembles a mob to break into the Sheriff's office, but they find Ruby's gone. Secretly, David's actually taken Ruby to the Library, where Belle begins to chain her up. However, Ruby tricks Belle and locks her up instead, saying that she's a monster and if the mob kills her, so be it.

David and Granny find a car with Ruby's cloak and a bloodied axe inside, and realize that Spencer framed Ruby. Hearing a howl, they head off to stop the mob from killing her. They find wolf-Ruby cornered by Spencer and the mob, and David tells the townspeople what Spencer did. Spencer admits to the murder and, dropping Jefferson's hat into a fire, gleefully says that he wants to watch David's face as he realizes he'll never see Snow and Emma again. Ruby has to restrain David from shooting Spencer – reminding him that he's a good guy.

Henry and Aurora both dream of the Netherworld again, but this time Henry uses the pendant to make the flames leap back and talks to her. She wakes up and tells a shocked Emma and Snow that she spoke to a boy called Henry…

## INTRODUCING:
This is the first time we meet Red's mother and fellow wolf, Anita (Annabeth Gish), as well as her companion, Quinn (Ben Hollingsworth).

## ONCE UPON A TIME…
Snow and Red are on the run from the Queen's men, but separate. Red meets a man, Quinn, and finds he's also a wolf. Quinn takes her to a lair where there are others like them, including a woman, Anita, who Red is shocked to find is her mother! Anita persuades Red that she must accept her wolf side, and teaches Red how to stay in control when she turns. Back at the lair, Quinn hears a noise – Snow has tracked Red there, and the Queen's men have followed her, where they kill Quinn. The wolves retaliate on the knights, and although Snow apologizes, Anita says that they're going to eat her too! Anita orders Red to kill Snow, but when she refuses, Anita and Red transform into wolves and fight. Red fatally wounds her mother, who rejects her for choosing Snow. Later, Red tells Snow that Anita wanted her to lose her human side, while Granny wanted her to reject her wolf side, but Snow's the only one who's accepted both.

## DID YOU NOTICE?
The title of the episode, "Child of the Moon" is the name of a Rolling Stones song, the B-side to their classic hit single "Jumping Jack Flash."

# 2.08 'Into the Deep'

**MR. GOLD:** "I HAVE A COMPLICATED RELATIONSHIP WITH HER. AS I DO WITH MOST PEOPLE."

Hook climbs down the beanstalk, only to be confronted by his erstwhile ally, Cora, who's angry that he failed her and decides to take matters into her own hands by using an enchanted heart to raise an army of undead warriors.

Emma and Mary Margaret realize that Aurora has been talking to Henry during her nightmares in the Netherworld, and when she sleeps again, she and Henry exchange information. When Henry wakes, he tells Regina that Emma and Snow need help to defeat Cora, much to Regina's shock.

Mr. Gold tells Regina, David and Henry about a weapon they can use against Cora – the magic ink from his cell in Fairy Tale Land. Back in the Netherworld, Henry tries to tell Aurora about the ink, but she's woken too soon – the camp is under attack from the undead! Cora captures Aurora and sends Snow and Emma her demands, saying that she'll trade her for the compass. Mulan wants to hand it over, but Snow and Emma want more time. Snow decides to visit the Netherworld herself to get the information from Henry. Hook lets himself into Aurora's cell and releases her, saying that if Emma can get him to Storybrooke, he'll steal the wardrobe ashes from Cora to create a portal. Troubled by Henry's burns from the Netherworld, David volunteers to undergo the sleeping curse so he can go instead, believing Snow will go there and can wake him with True Love's Kiss. Once under the curse, David forces his

way into the burning room, where he sees Snow. He tells her about the ink, but when they try to kiss to wake him from his sleeping curse, they realize they can't touch – their physical selves are still separated, and David will continue to be under the sleeping curse until Mary Margaret can get home to him. Mary Margaret and Emma decide to go after the ink, but Mulan has disappeared, taking the compass. They pursue her, but just as Mary Margaret threatens Mulan, Aurora appears, telling them that Hook helped her escape. However, we see what the women cannot: that Hook has given Aurora's heart to Cora, and Cora is using it to control her! The women go to find the ink, not realizing that Cora knows all of their plans!

## INTRODUCING:
This episode introduces us to a scary new side of Cora's magical powers – that she's able to reanimate the dead.

## ONCE UPON A TIME...
This episode features no flashbacks to times past.

## DID YOU NOTICE?
The idea of using a poppy to make someone sleep alludes to the poppy field in the classic book *The Wonderful Wizard of Oz*, which has a similar effect.

# 2.09 'Queen of Hearts'

**REGINA:** "THERE'S ONE PERSON I DON'T WANT FOLLOWING ME TO THIS NEW LAND."

In Storybrooke, David sleeps on, while Mr. Gold tells Regina that it could be Cora who comes through the portal, not Emma and Mary Margaret, and that they should destroy the portal. He pitches it as a win-win for Regina – no Emma and Mary Margaret, and no Cora. Although Regina is concerned about deceiving Henry, ultimately Gold is very convincing. Regina lies to Henry and says that she and Gold need to prepare for Emma and Margaret's return, when instead they go and steal the fairy dust from the mines to use to blow up the portal. When Ruby and Leroy find the fairy dust is missing they tell Henry, who realizes Regina lied to him.

In Fairy Tale Land present, Emma, Mary Margaret, Mulan, and Aurora search Rumplestiltskin's cell for the ink, but can't find it – just a scroll with Emma's name written over and over. Suddenly, Aurora locks the others in the cell, and Cora and Hook appear to confirm that Aurora is under their control! Cora takes the compass and Hook taunts Emma with a dried-up magic bean he stole from the Giant. Cora and Hook go to Lake Nostos so its magic can be used with the wardrobe ashes, and when they see that the lake's dried-up, Cora uses her powers

# 2.10 'The Cricket Game'

to create a geyser. She and Hook make a portal, while in Storybrooke, Regina and Gold enchant the well so anyone who comes through the portal will die!

Emma, Mary Margaret, and Mulan realize the magic ink is actually on the scroll, in the form of Emma's name, and use it to escape the dungeon. They quickly run to the lake, where they fight Cora and Hook, and manage to take the compass. During the battle, Hook shows a glimmer of goodness by returning Aurora's heart to Mulan. And when Cora tries to rip out Emma's heart, she is repelled by unexpected magic coming from inside Emma – and allowing Emma and Mary Margaret to escape and enter the portal to head home. Their plans apparently foiled, Cora and Hook create another portal using the dried-up magic bean in the water.

At the well, Henry pleads with Regina, until she relents and absorbs the enchantment that would kill anyone who comes through from Fairy Tale Land. Emma and Mary Margaret safely climb out of the well. Emma is stunned that Regina saved them, while Snow rushes to Gold's to wake David with True Love's Kiss. Henry departs with Emma, leaving Regina sad and dejected, and no one notices a pirate ship approaching Storybrooke from the sea... containing Cora and Hook. That's right, they used the water of Lake Nostos to revive the dried-up magic bean and create a second portal!

## INTRODUCING:

We'd met the Queen of Hearts in Season One's 'Hat Trick,' but her identity was hidden. In this episode, however, we find out who she truly is – Regina's mother, Cora.

## ONCE UPON A TIME...

We learn Regina and Hook have a past: she once enlisted his help, promising to kill Rumplestiltskin if he does something for her. The Evil Queen tells Hook she's about to enact a curse that will take them to a world without magic, where Hook could kill Rumplestiltskin, and all he has to do is kill someone for her – her mother. Hook goes to Wonderland and is brought before the Queen of Hearts, who turns out to be Cora! Cora turns Hook by pointing out that the curse will erase his memory of Fairy Tale Land and Rumplestiltskin – but she can help him get his revenge without forgetting who he is. In return, she needs his help to get close to Regina. Hook agrees and Cora uses magic to make herself appear dead to trick her daughter – and kill her when she least expects it. When Hook brings her body back, Regina surprises Cora by weeping over her body, and Cora changes her mind. Instead, Cora creates a protective spell around a small area in Fairy Tale Land when Regina unleashes her curse, so that she, Hook, and a few others are immune.

## DID YOU NOTICE?

The name Cora means "heart" in Latin – an entirely appropriate moniker for the Queen of Hearts!

## RUMPLESTILTSKIN: "REGINA REDEEMED! WHAT A NOVEL THOUGHT!"

Cora and Hook arrive in Storybrooke, but keep their presence secret – and Cora casts a cloaking spell over Hook's pirate ship. Hook wants to strike at Rumplestiltskin, but Cora reminds him that with magic in Storybrooke, it won't be easy, and that she has a plan to win Regina over to their side.

There's a welcome home party at Granny's for Emma and Mary Margaret, but when Regina arrives (invited by Emma), the townsfolk shun her. Although Emma is friendlier, she still rejects her request for time with Henry.

Regina continues her therapy sessions with Archie, but is angry when she finds out he told Emma about them. Ruby witnesses their argument, as does a hidden Cora. That night, Cora – disguised as Regina – goes to Archie's office and kills him. Archie's dog Pongo alerts Emma and Ruby, who find Archie's body. Helped by Mr. Gold, Emma uses her new-found magical power to witness Pongo's memories with a dreamcatcher, and sees Regina killing Archie. Emma tries to arrest Regina, but she escapes.

A heartbroken Regina later watches Emma tell Henry that she killed Archie. Meanwhile, Cora tells Hook that she has exactly what he needs to strike at Mr. Gold – she has the still living Archie imprisoned in the hold of his ship. Not only did she make herself look like Regina, she made an innocent bystander look like Archie and killed him instead. Hook prepares to interrogate Archie…

## INTRODUCING:
We don't meet many new characters in this episode, besides a fisherman (David Nykl) who makes the mistake of approaching Cora and Hook at the dock after he sees their ship and gets turned into a fish. Now there's a little poetic justice!

## ONCE UPON A TIME…
We see how Snow, Charming and their allies captured the Evil Queen and voted, despite Snow's misgivings, for her execution. Snow halts the execution, and Rumplestiltskin offers her a chance to test the Evil Queen. The Evil Queen fails the test, trying to kill Snow when given the opportunity, and is banished, with no power to harm Snow and Charming. Rumplestiltskin arrives at the Evil Queen's castle, however, and says that it's only in Fairy Tale Land that she cannot harm them – by manipulating her, Rumplestiltskin encourages her to use the Dark Curse and banish them all to Storybrooke, thus getting him closer to finding his son…

## DID YOU NOTICE?
The banner hanging in Granny's diner for the party is the same one used for Mary Margaret's release from jail in Season One's "The Stranger" (with the addition of Emma's name!).

# 2.11 'The Outsider'

**BELLE:** "WHEN YOU FIND SOMETHING WORTH FIGHTING FOR, YOU NEVER GIVE UP."

## INTRODUCING:
The title of the episode partly refers to Greg (Ethan Embry), who is technically introduced in this episode, when his car hits Hook, although we don't get to really know him until later in the season…

## ONCE UPON A TIME…
In Fairy Tale Land, we see Belle is desperate for adventure, and joins a quest to kill a monster, the Yaoguai. Soon out of her depth, she's saved by Mulan, and the two women team up. They track the Yaoguai and Belle uses fairy dust to transform the creature to its true form – Prince Philip. Philip and Mulan leave to save Aurora, while Belle sets off to see Rumplestiltskin, but is captured by the Evil Queen and her knights and tossed in a cell to be used as a bargaining tool.

## DID YOU NOTICE?
The outsider's car has Pennsylvania plates on it.

Mr. Gold tests the memory-robbing properties of the Storybrooke town line by enchanting Smee's hat and pushing him over it. Finding that his experiment has worked, he prepares to go and look for his son Baelfire, telling Belle that she can't come, as he can only enchant one more object.

Belle is menaced in her library by Hook, and Mr. Gold comes to save her, but when he does, Hook breaks into his shop and steals Baelfire's shawl, which Gold needs to cross the town line and find his son. Belle discovers Hook's hidden ship and releases Archie, but finds Hook with the shawl. Hook threatens her, but Mr. Gold comes to her rescue and begins to brutally beat Hook. Belle stops him, and Gold tells Hook to leave Storybrooke or he will kill him. Gold goes to the town line and enchants the shawl, but before he can leave town, Hook arrives and shoots Belle, who falls over the line and loses her memories. Gold prepares to kill Hook with a fireball when a car careens into view and hits Hook before crashing. A stranger has arrived in town…

# 2.12 'In the Name of the Brother'

## DR. WHALE/VICTOR: "I WANTED MY NAME TO STAND FOR LIFE. BUT EVERYBODY JUST THINKS IT'S THE NAME OF A MONSTER. I GUESS THEY WERE RIGHT ABOUT THAT."

Emma, Mary Margaret and David arrive at the scene of the accident, and Belle, Hook, and the stranger are taken to hospital to be treated by Dr. Whale. Whale is drunk, however, and doubts his abilities.

Cora visits Mr. Gold/Rumplestiltskin and offers a truce in return for a magic globe that will help him find his son. They kiss "like they used to" to seal the deal. Cora then disguises herself as Henry and finds Regina hiding in her vault. Cora reveals herself to her daughter. At first, Regina demands that Cora confess to the murder she was framed for, but relents when Cora says that she can help get Henry back.

Gold desperately tries to retrieve Belle's memories by enchanting her chipped cup, but she smashes it. Devastated, he leaves with the globe to find his son, who he discovers is in New York City.

Dr. Whale contemplates ending it all, but is talked out of it by Ruby, who bonds with him. Whale goes back to the hospital and saves the life of the stranger, who on being questioned says that he didn't see anything unusual occur. Gold goes to Emma to call in the favor she owes him – she's going to New York with him to help find Baelfire, immediately! Meanwhile, the stranger talks on the phone to an unknown woman and says he won't believe what he's seen…

## INTRODUCING:
We'd previously seen Dr. Frankenstein's brother Gerhardt in "The Doctor," but this is the first time we meet their father Alphonse (Gregory Itzin). He's not the most sympathetic father, and suffers for it in the end!

## ONCE UPON A TIME…
We see more of the history of Dr. Whale's alter-ego, Dr. Victor Frankenstein. We learn that his father Alphonse celebrated his soldier brother Gerhardt, but was indifferent to scientist Victor, and eventually disinherits him. As Victor packs up, Rumplestiltskin appears and promises to teach him how to bring back the dead in return for gold. When Victor robs a grave for a suitable specimen, Gerhardt arrives to stop him and is shot dead by a watchman. Victor becomes determined to bring Gerhardt back, but fails until Rumplestiltskin helps him trick Regina to get an enchanted heart. Gerhardt is brought back and Alphonse is delighted, until he realizes that Gerhardt is mindless – a mere shadow of his former self. He berates Victor, but the reanimated Gerhardt beats their father to death. Victor tries to kill Gerhardt, but can't, and vows to save him instead…

## DID YOU NOTICE?
Greg's ringtone is the theme from the movie *Star Wars*.

# 2.13 'Tiny'

## ANTON: "I'M TOO SMALL FOR BACK HOME. I'M TOO BIG FOR HERE."

Emma gets ready to leave for New York with Gold and takes Henry with her – she won't leave him behind with Regina and Cora on the loose. Gold's enchanted shawl works and he's able to keep his memories when he leaves Storybrooke.

As David and Mary Margaret search for Cora, they are visited by Regina and tell her that they know Cora committed the murder Regina was accused of – and that Henry's left town with Emma. David and Mary Margaret go with a semi-recovered Hook to the *Jolly Roger*, where Hook reveals that Cora's plans involve another captive – the Giant, whom Cora has shrunk to human size. They free him, but when the Giant sees David, he angrily attacks, telling a confused David that he'll make him pay for his evil!

David realizes that his late twin, Prince James, must have done something to arouse the Giant's ire. Regina tracks the Giant to the woods offers to help him grow back to giant size in return for his allegiance; he accepts, and Regina casts the spell. The now giant Giant rampages through town, and just as he's about to squash David, he shrinks again, and is left hanging over a crevasse. The townspeople save him, and tell him that he's welcome to stay – and that there's no way back to Fairy Tale Land. The Giant surprises them all by producing a piece of beanstalk and says that he can grow a new field of magic beans – that's what Cora wanted him for. The Dwarfs give Anton a pickaxe like theirs, and the name "Tiny" appears on it before they start to cultivate a new beanfield together.

Meanwhile, Greg and Belle confer at the hospital and confirm that they both witnessed magic...

## INTRODUCING:

We'd already met the Giant, Anton (Jorge Garcia), in "Tallahassee," and in this episode we meet his wiser brother Arlo (Abraham Benrubi). We also meet Jack the Giant Killer (Cassidy Freeman) who, in a fun twist on the original tale, is actually a beautiful woman.

## ONCE UPON A TIME...

We learn more about the Giant, Anton. A bit of a misfit amongst his own, he spies on humans, wanting to be like them. Prince James and his lady friend Jack use this to their advantage, helping Anton shrink down to human size with some enchanted mushrooms. But it's all part of a nefarious plot to get their hands on some magic beans, which the giants

cultivate – and James and Jack end up turning on Anton and attacking his people, slaying them all with poisoned swords. Before Anton's older brother dies, he begs him to raze the fields so that the evil humans won't be able to take the beans and use them to their advantage. Jack is killed in the fight and James absconds with some of the treasure that the giants have been hoarding. With his last dying breath, Anton's brother gives him a piece of beanstalk, telling him that he'll find a new land someday...

## DID YOU NOTICE?

When Anton and the Dwarfs are digging, they are whistling the song "Heigh Ho" from the classic animated movie *Snow White and the Seven Dwarfs*.

# 2.14 'Manhattan'

## MR. GOLD: "THERE'S NO GREATER PAIN THAN REGRET." NEAL: "TRY ABANDONMENT."

Mr. Gold, Emma, and Henry track Rumplestiltskin's son Baelfire to an apartment building in Manhattan, but when they ring his bell, they hear him making a run for it. Emma pursues and tackles the man, and finds to her shock that he's Neal Cassidy – her former love, and Henry's father! Neal takes her to a bar to talk, where she makes it clear how angry she is at him for deserting her. Neal tells Emma that he doesn't want to see his father and asks her to pretend she lost him.

Emma calls Mary Margaret for advice, telling her that Gold is Henry's grandfather. Mary Margaret tells her that she should remember how important it is to know who your parents are, and that Henry should be told about Neal. Emma ignores her advice, returns to Gold and Henry, and says that she lost the man. Gold,

desperate to find his son, breaks into Neal's apartment, and Emma finds an old dreamcatcher from her days with Neal. Neal returns to his apartment and agrees to talk to Gold after meeting his son, Henry – and Henry's disappointed that Emma lied to him about his father.

Meanwhile, in Storybrooke, Regina, Cora, and Hook go on a hunt for Gold's enchanted dagger. A clue in Belle's purse leads them to the library, where they find a map inside a book. Hook finds the dagger's location on the map, but Cora casts him aside with her magic, saying that the dagger's too useful to be wasted on him. Cora tells Regina she wants the Dark One's power so they can kill their enemies and return Henry to Regina.

And back in the hospital, Greg has captured footage of magic in Storybrooke and called his mysterious contact...

# 2.15 'The Queen is Dead'

RUMPLESTILTSKIN: "IT'S A SAD TRUTH THAT THE PEOPLE CLOSEST TO US ARE THE ONES CAPABLE OF CAUSING US THE MOST PAIN."

## INTRODUCING:
We meet the Seer, played by Brighid Fleming as a little girl, and Shannon Lucio as an adult. Although we'd met Henry's father Neal Cassidy before, in this episode, we finally discover that he's really Rumplestiltskin's son, Baelfire.

## ONCE UPON A TIME...
Early in his marriage, we see Rumplestiltskin being called up to fight in the Ogre Wars, keen to prove that he isn't a coward. Once in the army, he's ordered to guard something in a cage. Curious, he looks inside to find a girl with her eyelids stitched up and eyes on her palms. She says that she's a Seer, and predicts that his wife Milah is pregnant and that his actions on the battlefield will leave the child fatherless. The next day, he finds proof that she was telling the truth, and injures his own leg with a hammer in order to avoid the battle. Returning home, he finds a very disappointed Milah, and we now know why she called him a coward. Later, as the Dark One, Rumplestiltskin confronts the Seer again, and learns that he'll find his lost son after many years pass. He also finds out that the boy who helps him find Bae will be his undoing. Rumplestiltskin says that in that case he'll have to kill the boy – Henry!

## DID YOU NOTICE?
The title card for the episode features the Manhattan skyline.

In New York City, Henry and his father Neal/Baelfire are taking some time to bond when Hook appears and plunges a poisoned hook deep into Gold's chest. Emma quickly knocks the pirate out, but too late: Gold realizes that this is no ordinary wound, and only the magic back in Storybrooke can save him. They must get there as soon as possible and there's only one way to do that –Hook's *Jolly Roger*. To everyone's surprise, Neal seems to know Hook – and somewhere along his journey from Fairy Tale Land to New York City, learned how to steer his ship. But before they leave, Neal has one more surprise in store for Emma: he's engaged!

Back in Storybrooke we learn that it's Mary Margaret's birthday and she receives a present from her beloved Fairy Tale Land maid, Johanna: a tiara her mother gave her as a child. Mary Margaret finds her old friend in a secluded house and they reunite, when Mary Margaret hears a noise in the woods and goes to investigate. She overhears Regina and Cora talking about their search for Rumplestiltskin's dagger, and how they'll use it to make Rumplestiltskin kill their enemies – including her, David and Emma! Mary Margaret and David call Emma, who's with Rumplestiltskin, and track down the dagger first.

They find the dagger cleverly hidden behind the hand of the clock at the tower, but as soon as it's in their possession Cora and Regina magically appear, with Johanna as bait. Regina tears out Johanna's heart and tortures her until Mary Margaret gives in and hands the dagger over. Cora kills Johanna anyway, pushing her out the high tower window.

Distraught at the death of another maternal figure, Snow decides that being good has caused her and those she loves nothing but pain... so now she will kill Cora!

## INTRODUCING:
For the first time we meet Snow's mother, Eva (Rena Sofer), a benevolent queen, as well as her faithful maidservant, Johanna (Lesley Nicol).

## ONCE UPON A TIME...
In Fairy Tale Land past, we see the young Snow being taught how to be a good and future queen by her mother, Eva. When Eva suddenly falls mortally ill, her maid Johanna tells Snow that only one person can save her: the Blue Fairy. The Blue Fairy tells Snow that only the darkest of magic can bring her mother back from the brink of death, and gives Snow a magical candle that will save her mother's life... at the cost of another's. Snow simply can't do it, and goes tearfully to her mother's bedside, where her mother tells her she's so proud of her for taking the good path – and that as long as good is in her heart she will be with her. Eva dies, and after the funeral, the Blue Fairy appears, and reveals that it was actually Cora in disguise!

## DID YOU NOTICE?
Eva's bedchamber is the same one later used by Regina once she becomes queen.

# 2.16 'The Miller's Daughter'

CORA: "ROYAL BRIDES HAVE TO BE SNOW WHITE."
RUMPLESTILTSKIN: "WHEN YOU CAN SEE THE FUTURE, THERE'S IRONY EVERYWHERE."

The *Jolly Roger* docks in Storybrooke, and Emma, David, Mary Margaret, and Neal take the critically injured Mr. Gold to his shop. Meanwhile, Cora tells Regina that rather than use Rumplestiltskin's dagger to control him, she thinks she should use it to kill him and become the Dark One herself. Regina begins to suspect that getting Henry back isn't her mother's true motive…

Our heroes barricade themselves and Gold in his shop, and he helps Emma use her newfound magic powers to cast a protection spell on the door. Gold tricks Mary Margaret into finding the candle Cora gave her (while disguised as the Blue Fairy) when she was a child. He tries to persuade her to use it to save him by killing Cora – all she need do is whisper Cora's name as she burns the candle over Cora's heart, which Cora has hidden away somewhere. Cora and Regina break into the shop and battle the heroes, while Mary Margaret slips away to find Cora's heart. Emma holds Regina at swordpoint, forcing Cora to choose between grabbing the dagger, or helping her daughter… and Cora chooses the dagger. Emma and Neal escape to the back room and magically seal its entrance, while

Cora senses something is amiss with her heart and sends Regina after it.

The dying Gold calls Belle and tells her how he feels about her, even though she doesn't remember him, and Emma and Neal are touched by his tender words. Meanwhile, in Regina's vault, Mary Margaret lights the candle over Cora's heart and whispers her name! On her way out, she runs into Regina, and takes the opportunity to trick the evil queen, by telling her that Cora could never truly love her daughter without her heart – and gives Cora's heart to Regina.

Back at Mr. Gold's, Cora breaks through to the back room and magically banishes Emma and Neal. Approaching Gold, Cora tells him she had to remove her own heart because she loved him, and it was her weakness. Just as she's about to kill him with his dagger, Regina thrusts Cora's heart back into her body! Cora looks on her daughter with true love for the first time before she collapses. Realizing what an evil deed she's done, Mary Margaret rushes to the scene to warn Regina – but it is too late. Gold magically recovers as Cora dies, and Regina now hates Snow White more than ever!

## INTRODUCING:

We meet the younger Cora (Rose McGowan), a fiery and fiercely ambitious miller's daughter, as well as King Xavier (Joaqium de Almeida) and his son Prince Henry (Zak Santiago), Regina's father.

## ONCE UPON A TIME…

We learn Cora's backstory. The daughter of a drunken miller, she's forced to humiliate herself in front of the king's court. Later, gatecrashing a ball, she flirts with the king's son Henry, and when she's called out as a simple miller's daughter, Cora brags that she can spin straw into gold. The king takes the opportunity to lock her in a tower to prove it. In her despair, Cora is visited by Rumplestiltskin, who says he can spin the gold in return for her first-born, but Cora says no – she wants him to teach her how to do it herself. Rumplestiltskin accepts. The next day, Cora succeeds in her task in front of the king and becomes betrothed to the prince as her reward. However, Cora and Rumplestiltskin have fallen in love and plan to run away together, altering their bargain so that their price is their first-born child together. But first Cora wants to teach the king a lesson, and asks Rumplestiltskin to show her how to take a heart. The king, however, offers her a different kind of bargain: give up her love for real power. When Cora goes to meet Rumplestiltskin with a heart in a casket, it's her own – she's removed it so she won't be tempted by love, and tells him she's going to marry the prince.

## DID YOU NOTICE?

While speaking on the phone, Mary Margaret nervously plays with a red apple – not unlike the one Regina used to put her under the sleeping curse back in Fairy Tale Land.

# 2.17 'Welcome to Storybrooke'

**MR. GOLD:** "CORA WAS A DANGEROUS WOMAN BECAUSE SHE DIDN'T HAVE A HEART. REGINA IS EVEN MORE DANGEROUS BECAUSE SHE *DOES*."

R egina is mourning the death of Cora in the mausoleum when Mr. Gold arrives with a rose for her grave. He expresses his own sadness, but Regina rejects him for his part in her mother's death and says Mary Margaret will pay as well for tricking her into killing Cora. Gold tries to convince her that the curse did not make her happy, and nor will vengeance. He says she will lose Henry if she is bent on revenge, but Regina says she'll have both. After he leaves, a distraught Regina tears the room apart and discovers a curse hidden in her mother's dress.

At Mary Margaret's apartment, Emma is forced by Henry to admit that Mary Margaret killed Cora, which stuns the little boy. Mr. Gold arrives with news of Regina's plans and he's coerced into helping them. David and Mr. Gold return to the mausoleum and find Regina has taken potion ingredients to make the Curse of the Broken Hearted, which can make someone love you. Back at the apartment, Henry is worried Regina will use the potion on him, but Mr. Gold explains it's more complicated: Regina needs the heart of the

person she hates most to enact the curse and that would be Mary Margaret's heart.

Henry doesn't want any harm to come to Regina, but Emma asks him to go live with Neal so he won't be a pawn in Regina's plan. Henry suggests they destroy magic instead and excuses himself to the bathroom. Emma and Neal quickly figure out Henry made a run for it. In the woods, Henry runs into Greg Mendell on a hike, and he calls Regina to pick up her son.

Regina attempts to acquire Mary Margaret's heart, but Mr. Gold stops her using his own magic. She heads out to get Henry, who is at the wishing well intent on obliterating the magic he says is breaking apart his family. Emma, David and Neal arrive, and it gets ugly between the warring factions. Henry screams that magic is what makes good people do bad things, and his plea makes everyone stand down.

Later Mary Margaret asks Regina to kill her for recompense, but Regina declines, for Henry's sake. Instead she takes out Mary Margaret's heart and shows her there's a black spot on it now and that it will eventually destroy her, and that will be Regina's true revenge.

## INTRODUCING:

Previously, we met Greg Mendell (Ethan Embry) in "Tiny," but in this episode we discover he's really Owen Flynn, the son of kidnapped Kurt Flynn (John Pyper-Ferguson).

## ONCE UPON A TIME...

This episode, the flashback is to 1983 and the first day post-curse in Storybrooke. Regina's practically giddy that all of her Fairy Tale Land foes are now blissfully ignorant of their past lives and living new identities. That is until she quickly gets bored with the repetition of her bland new life. She turns her attention to Kurt and Owen Flynn, a father and son, who somehow stumble into town to get their car repaired. Intrigued, Regina turns on the charm. She wins Owen's favor, and the two try to convince Kurt to relocate to Storybrooke permanently. Kurt declines, but Regina doesn't like the word no, so she orders Sheriff Graham to arrest him for drunk driving before they escape the town limits. Owen is aghast at Regina's dark plan and escapes into the woods. Sometime later, he returns to the town limits with police, but there's no Storybrooke to be seen. Owen vows to get his father back.

## DID YOU NOTICE?

There is an advertisement on a bench for ENCOM – the software company featured in the *Tron* movies. The sequel *Tron: Legacy* was written by Once Upon a Time creators Eddy Kitsis and Adam Horowitz. Also, Kurt and Owen's last name, Flynn, is the same is that of Kevin and Sam Flynn – the father and son protagonists in the *Tron* movies.

# 2.18 'Selfless, Brave and True'

## INTRODUCING:

Neal introduces everyone to his fiancée Tamara (played by Sonequa Martin-Green), whom we, and Emma, met briefly in "The Queen is Dead." We also meet The Dragon (Tzi Ma).

## ONCE UPON A TIME...

The flashback revolves solely around August Booth's checkered past. In 2011, Booth wakes up with a beautiful woman, only to discover his leg is wooden and he's reverting back to his previous state. At a hospital, the doctor only sees normal skin, so August stabs his leg to prove otherwise. Appalled, the doctor tries to commit him. August runs to escape and a man pulls him aside to tell him that "The Dragon" can solve his problem for a price.

In The Dragon's waiting room, August meets Tamara. Inside The Dragon's den, the man identifies August as Pinocchio and says he can reverse his problem for the price of August's necklace from his father and ten thousand dollars. Lacking the funds, he leaves and runs into Tamara at a bar. They exchange stories and when she's distracted, he steals money from her purse to pay The Dragon. August pays for the "cure," but once outside is pursued by Tamara. He drops the vial he'd been given, and is left in tears. But it turns out that Tamara is a true charlatan and she kills The Dragon for his otherworldly cures, then follows August back to New York to orchestrate her own meeting with Neal.

## REGINA: "CONTRARY TO WHAT YOU MIGHT BELIEVE, PEOPLE CAN JUST DISAPPEAR."

Still reeling from her role in Cora's death, Mary Margaret decides to go into the woods to process everything that's happened recently. While practicing her archery skills an odd sound draws her to August Booth's trailer, where she sees he's regressed to his wooden state. He tells her this is his punishment for his deceit, and he asks about his father. Mary Margaret tries to get him to come back to town, but he refuses and asks her not to tell anyone where he is hiding.

Meanwhile at Granny's, Neal tells Emma Hook has escaped and his fiancée, Tamara, is Storybrooke bound. Soon after, Tamara arrives and things get pretty awkward. Henry asks how he met Neal and Tamara tells him they literally bumped into one another. After Henry exits, Neal takes the opportunity to show Tamara Henry's storybook and to reveal he is really Baelfire of the Enchanted Forest. She doesn't believe him, and thinks there is something still going on between him and Emma.

Regina runs into Greg Mendell and she realizes that this man is little Owen Flynn all grown up. She tells Greg that his father left Storybrooke long ago, but he says he doesn't

believe her and that he'll stay. Regina is not pleased and she not-so-subtly threatens to make him disappear.

Back in town, Mary Margaret tells Marco about August's predicament, and they decide to approach Mother Superior for her help. All the while, Tamara is listening and heads to August's trailer in the woods. She offers him the cure he dropped years ago in exchange for his leaving Storybrooke for good. Tempted, August is in the car, heading out of town, when he discovers the photo Tamara gave as payment to The Dragon, prompting him to go to the Sheriff's office and call Emma for help. Tamara shows up in a rage and attacks him with the same anti-magic device she used to kill The Dragon. Emma, Marco and Mary Margaret arrive just in time for him to expire in Marco's arms. Henry recalls the Blue Fairy's magical words and Mother Superior shows up with her wand to turn August into a real boy – Pinocchio. He wakes with no memory of Tamara's nefarious intentions.

After the drama, Tamara meets Greg on the sly and the two kiss – revealing that they are working together!

## DID YOU NOTICE?

August has a necklace with the image of a whale on it – a reference to Monstro the whale, who we met in Season One's "The Stranger."

# 2.19 'Lacey'

## LACEY: "YOU CAN'T TELL WHAT'S IN A PERSON'S HEART UNLESS YOU TRULY KNOW THEM."

**M**r. Gold awakens from a life-like dream in which he turns Henry into stone and smashes him to pieces in order to prevent the Seer's prophecy. Later, he tells Regina that Henry is Neal's son, and that he is Henry's grandfather. She thinks he orchestrated Henry's adoption, but he says it was only fate.

Struggling with the prophecy, Mr. Gold visits Belle in the hospital. He admits that he has true feelings for her, which she seems to believe. He tells her he will help her get her memory back so she can help him be a better man.

When Mr. Gold leaves to get Belle discharged, Regina arrives and introduces herself as the mayor. With her magic, she enchants a matchbook from The Rabbit Hole and has Belle stare at it, which jogs the young woman's memory. When Mr. Gold returns, Belle's room is empty and he sees the matchbook from the bar. He arrives there asking for Belle and is directed instead to a transformed woman, a barfly who responds to the name Lacey.

Meanwhile, in secret, Greg and Tamara plot together over a map of Storybrooke. They track the places where they've witnessed magic and discuss the possible places they might find Greg's father, Kurt.

Outside the town, David and Mary Margaret pull Emma through an invisibility cloak to see the protected magic beanfield. A shrunken Anton is tending the field under Leroy's supervision. They explain to Emma that Mother Superior cloaked the fields to protect the crop so they can return to their land and perhaps give Emma her happy ending in the Enchanted Forest after all.

Mr. Gold confronts Regina about what she did to Belle, and she admits that Belle was given back her cursed memories and Lacey is here to stay. Gold seeks David's counsel, who advises him to remind Belle of the man she fell in love with in the first place.

Determined to bring back the Belle he loves with True Love's kiss, Gold takes Lacey on a date to Granny's Diner. Though things seem to go well at first, Gold soon discovers Lacey is more interested in Keith, the former Sheriff of Nottingham.

At the same time, Regina begins to suspect the Charmings are keeping something from her. Using magic, she is able to trace their recent activity, leading her to the bean field.

In a fit of despair, Gold corners Keith and beats him savagely, only to discover Lacey has seen the whole thing. Far from being frightened, Lacey is attracted to Gold's more dangerous persona, and so he resumes the beating.

Finally, Greg meets Tamara at the town line where she reveals the identity of her secret package: Hook!

## INTRODUCING:

We meet the tortured thief known as Robin Hood (played by Tom Ellis), who is freed from Rumplestiltskin's death sentence by Belle. We also meet the thief's lover, Marian (Christie Laing), who is pregnant with his child, and the Sheriff of Nottingham (Will Traval), who hates the thief for winning Marian from him.

## ONCE UPON A TIME...

Not long into Belle's servitude for Rumplestiltskin, he callously complains about her crying and gifts her with a pillow to muffle her sobs. A thief then breaks into the keep to steal a magic wand using an enchanted bow that always finds its target. It does (target: Rumple), but the arrow does nothing more than to annoy the giddy villain. Rumplestiltskin then tortures the thief in another room while Belle listens to the man's screams of agony. Taking a break from his work, Rumplestiltskin orders Belle to clean his bloody apron and explains that anyone who steals from him will be flayed alive. Belle helps the thief escape and doesn't join him because she feels she must honor her agreement to serve in order to save her family.

Furious, Rumplestiltskin sets out to hunt the thief and brings Belle along to watch. However, when he discovers the man, who turns out to be Robin Hood, stole the wand to heal his pregnant wife, Rumple lets him go. As they return to Rumple's keep, Belle begins to see her captor in a new light for the first time.

## DID YOU NOTICE?

The thief's arrow is featured in the episode's title card graphic.

173

# 2.20 'The Evil Queen'

**REGINA:** "WHEN SNOW IS DEAD, THEN THEY WILL SEE MY KINDNESS."
**RUMPLESTILTSKIN:** "THROUGH THE CHARRED REMAINS OF THEIR HOMES? YES, I'M SURE THAT WILL BE PERFECTLY CLEAR."

Having discovered the magic beanfield, Regina overhears David and Mary Margaret talking about her planned fate: either to stay behind in Storybrooke alone, or to return with them, but live out her existence in Rumplestiltskin's old cell. Neither option is acceptable to Regina, so she plans her own Option C.

Meanwhile, Greg and Tamara take the captive Hook to the Storybrooke clock tower, where they show him that Rumplestiltskin is still alive. They appear to convince an angry Hook to help them find Greg's father and to wipe out magic for good. They release him and he heads straight to Regina's office, where he shares the duo's plan and says he prefers to work with her instead. Regina grins and shares her own plan to destroy Rumplestiltskin. Together they enter the caverns under the town and Regina spies Hook wearing the cuff Cora gave to him. Livid, Regina demands he hand it over to her,

which he does. She then throws him into a pit to distract a re-formed Maleficent, while she goes to retrieves the curse "fail safe," a black diamond, from Snow's coffin. Regina leaves Hook to escape on his own.

At Granny's Diner, Emma runs into Tamara, who tries to sell her trustworthiness – something Emma's lie-detecting power isn't buying. Henry also doesn't believe Tamara, so he and Emma set up a stakeout. As they wait, Emma accidentally lets slip about the Enchanted Forest plan, and Henry approves. They then snoop in Tamara's room but are busted by Neal and are further embarrassed when her room reveals nothing incriminating. Drat!

Back in the library, Hook is waiting for Regina, having escaped his fate with the help of Greg and Tamara. Regina is ready to unleash some magic... but nothing happens. The duo used science via Cora's cuff to squash Regina's powers, and now she's at their mercy.

## INTRODUCING:
We meet a brand new zombie-like version of Maleficent, who still guards the "fail safe" pit beneath Storybrooke.

## ONCE UPON A TIME...
Snow White is still on the run and the Evil Queen is hot on her heels. At a village Snow recently left, the Queen assembles the residents and demands they tell her where Snow went, but they remain silent. She has her soldiers wipe out the entire village as punishment. Back at her castle, she has Rumplestiltskin cast a transformation spell on her so she can hide amongst the people as a commoner. However, under the spell she won't have her magic, and will need to call for Rumplestiltskin if she's in peril.

Out amongst the people, the Evil Queen sees how much the people hate her and love Snow. She even interrupts a game where the people can shoot arrows through the Queen's visage. When two of the Queen's soldiers see the game, they pull the Queen (still disguised as a commoner) out of the crowd for execution, but Snow saves her life at the last second. Snow takes the Queen to her hideout and dresses her wounds. For a few days, they bond in peace, with Snow even admitting that she wants to forgive the Queen... until they come across the remains of the village the Evil Queen decimated. Snow then realizes her companion has been the Queen all along, but she can't kill her. The Queen runs to Rumplestiltskin's home, where he magically lifts her disguise. With a heavy heart, she finally accepts she can only rule through fear and intimidation.

## DID YOU NOTICE?
In return for shifting her shape, Rumple asks Regina to cut off all trade with King George's realm. Eventually, this will render George's kingdom bankrupt, setting the stage for George's alliance with Midas, and the meeting of Charming and Snow White.

# 2.21 'Second Star to the Right'

## BAELFIRE: "MAGIC IS DANGEROUS. IT ALWAYS COMES WITH A PRICE."

### INTRODUCING:
We meet the Darling children of *Peter Pan* lore: Wendy (Freya Tingley), John (William Ainschough) and Michael (Benjamin Cook).

### ONCE UPON A TIME...

The flash to the past this time continues Baelfire's journey after he enters the portal and turns up in Victorian London. Homeless and starving, he breaks into the Darling home to steal some bread, where he meets Wendy Darling, who promises to help him. Eventually, Wendy's parents discover Bae too, and invite him to stay with them. Wendy shares with Bae that a magical shadow comes to visit her at night, which he begs her to ignore. Instead, she lets the shadow spirit her away past the second star to the right. Wendy returns the next morning upset to have learned that Neverland is a nightmarish place you can never leave. She says it only let her go because it wants a boy, and will return to steal one of her brothers, John or Michael, that night. When it returns, Bae offers himself in exchange and as he and the shadow approach Neverland, Bae strikes a match, which startles the shadow. It drops Baelfire, who is then fished out of the sea by Captain Hook!

### DID YOU NOTICE?

Baelfire lands in London's Kensington Gardens, which is the setting for J. M. Barrie's prequel *Peter Pan* story, *Peter Pan in Kensington Gardens*.

reg and Tamara ready to torture Regina, using a larger version of the anti-magic device Tamara used to neutralize August, to make her reveal Kurt's whereabouts. Tamara also sends information back to her secret collaborators about the magic beans and the black diamond.

Regina's absence puts Emma and company on alert, and they decide to fan out to track her down. David and Mary Margaret head to Mr. Gold's, while Emma returns to Tamara's hotel room. She tells Neal about her concerns and when they find sand in the closet, where Tamara keeps her running shoes, they make for the beach to investigate.

Mr. Gold is hanging out with Lacey and doesn't want to help, but David says he owes him a favor. Gold concocts a potion that allows Mary Margaret to share experiences with Regina. Once taken, Mary Margaret feels Regina's painful torture in a cold, dark place that smells like sardines. David calls Emma and Neal who are at the beach together, and they figure out Regina is being held in the Storybrooke Cannery – voila!

Tamara gets wind they have visitors and heads out to stop them, while Greg gives Regina one last chance to tell the truth. She finally admits she killed Kurt and buried the body at his campsite. Greg is incensed and he cranks up the juice on the machine, intending to kill Regina, but is stopped in the nick of time by David. Greg gets away while David and Mary Margaret whisk Regina to Mother Superior for healing.

Meanwhile, Tamara sneaks up on Emma and knocks her out, tells Neal their relationship is a fraud and then shoots him. Emma recovers and regains the gun from Tamara, but Tamara drops a magic bean, which opens a portal that sucks Neal to its edge! Panicked, Emma grabs onto him, but her grip is no match for the whirlwind. Neal tells her to let go for Henry's sake and that he loves her, then lets go and once again disappears into a portal. Heartbroken, Emma reunites with her parents and Regina, at which point they all realize the diamond is no longer in their possession. At the campsite, Greg and Tamara find Kurt's remains and their collaborators tell them to initiate the next phase of their plan: Storybrooke's destruction!

## INTRODUCING:

We witness the unexpected reintroduction of Aurora (Sarah Bolger), Mulan (Jamie Chung) and Philip (Julian Morris) in the last moments of the episode, when they discover Neal on a beach!

## HENRY: "WE DON'T LEAVE FAMILY BEHIND."

**G**reg and Tamara engage the "fail safe," dooming anyone from Fairy Tale Land to die as the forest consumes Storybrooke. Regina offers to help slow the process, so she can buy time for David to retrieve a magic bean that will open a portal back to the Enchanted Forest. Even Hook is helping; it's only a despondent Mr. Gold who is ready to meet his end as he mourns the loss of his son Bae.

David and Hook track down Greg and Tamara. There's a physical confrontation, but both parties end up with a bean and go their separate ways. At the same time, Emma discovers that Regina must sacrifice her own life to slow down the black diamond. Emma, Henry, David and Mary Margaret decide they can't let that happen, and devise a plan to jettison the fail safe through a portal with their bean. Hook disagrees with the plan at first, but relents and hands Emma the pouch.

In the mines, Regina's magic is being overwhelmed, when Emma discovers Hook stole the bean and is sailing away on the *Jolly Roger*. Emma decides to try merging her own magic

with Regina's to save the town. Together, the two women blow out the fail safe and Storybrooke is saved. The only problem is that in the chaos Greg and Tamara have kidnapped Henry!

Elsewhere, the dwarves finally cure Sneezy's memory loss, and Leroy leaves an extra dose of the cure to Mr. Gold so he can restore Belle's real memories. Initially he balks, but decides he'd rather die with the woman he loves (Belle, not Lacey), and they have an emotional reunion.

At the docks, Greg and Tamara reveal their collaborator is more interested in Henry, so they use their bean to disappear before Emma and family can save the day. In the distance, Belle sees Hook's *Jolly Roger* coming back to help the town. He offers his ship and the bean as a means to find Henry. Hook welcomes Emma, Mary Margaret, David, Regina and even Mr. Gold onboard for an epic rescue mission to find Henry. Belle meanwhile stays behind to cloak Storybrooke from outsiders once more. Mr. Gold then produces Cora's magic globe and it reveals Henry is in Neverland. Gold realizes who their real enemy is – Peter Pan – as they sail into the portal for Neverland.

## ONCE UPON A TIME...

We're back to Neverland right after Hook fishes Baelfire out of the drink and brings him aboard the *Jolly Roger*. Upset about being saved by a pirate (and not knowing he's the one who destroyed his family), Bae is hostile towards Hook. Yet the pirate knows who the boy is and promises to offer him sanctuary from Peter Pan and the Lost Boys. Surprisingly, Bae settles into life on the ship and even warms to Hook until he spies a picture of his mother on the Captain's desk and the young boy puts everything together. Hook tells Bae the truth – that Rumplestiltskin killed Milah. Regardless, Bae wants off the *Jolly Roger* and so Hook hands him over to the Lost Boys.

## DID YOU NOTICE?

Emma, for the first time ever in the series, calls Snow and David "Mom and Dad."